St. Patrick's Cathedral

St. Patrick's Cathedral

By
LELAND A. COOK

Foreword by
TERENCE CARDINAL COOKE

Introduction by
BRENDAN GILL

New York London Tokyo

International Standard Book Numbers:
0-8256-3158-0 (paperbound)
0-8256-3169-6 (hardcover)

Library of Congress Catalog Card
Number: 79-88702

In Great Britain: Book Sales Ltd., 78
Newman Street, London WIP 3LA,
England

In Canada: Gage Trade Publishing,
P.O. Box 5000, 164 Commander Blvd.,
Agincourt, Ontario M1S 3C7, Canada

In Japan: Quick Fox, 4-26-22 Jingumae,
Shibuya-Ku, Tokyo 150, Japan

Book design by Frances Greenberg
Cover design by Iris Weinstein
Cover photograph by David Frazier

I wish to thank the following people for their
encouragement and cooperation to make this a
successful publication.

His Eminence Terence Cardinal Cooke
Reverend Monsignor James F. Rigney,
    Rector of St. Patrick's Cathedral
Reverend Charles J. Mahoney, C.S.C.
Ms. Grace Bruce
Dick Cassidy
Ms. Penny Ryan
Brendan Gill
Ms. Andrea Thompson
William Thompson
Herbert Wise
David Frazier
Barbara Kelman-Burgower
Frances Greenberg
Christopher Grey
Jeanette Mall
Bernard Carroll
Richard Yosca
Ms. Josephine Dioguardi
Mrs. Joanne Baher
Andrew Kroh
Grant Jeffery
Naomi & Donald De Lue
Gertrude Neidlinger
Travis Neidlinger
James Charlton

Dedicated to my wife Sunny
and to Kathy and Kit

Contents

Overleaf: Celebration of mass on the 100th birthday of St. Patrick's Cathedral, May, 1979.

Foreword

by Terence Cardinal Cooke

A hundred years ago, Fifth Avenue and Fiftieth Street was largely a rural setting. The new Cathedral of St. Patrick rose tall and solitary. In fact, when the spires were completed, it is reported that they could be seen from a distance of twenty miles.

The United States was a very young country in 1879. There were people whose parents had lived here under the British flag. The population of 49,000,000 Americans was still excited by the realization that for ten years it had been possible to cross the country by railroad. The telephone was a three year old invention; carriage making was a million dollar a year business, employing 75,000 people who produced about a million carriages a year.

The population of New York City, according to the census of 1870, was 942,000 people. This figure was then customarily divided into a native population of 523,000 and a so-called foreign population of 419,000. There were large numbers of people from England, France, Germany, Ireland and Scotland, as well as lesser numbers from a great number of other nations.

There were but two economic classes — the poor and the rich. Living in New York in 1879 was so expensive that even people of moderate means lived outside the city, some of them as far as forty miles out into the countryside. Comtemporary accounts of the city's prosperity in 1879 mentioned with pride 420 miles of streets, 1,900 gas lamps, 400 miles of water-main and the fact that the City's public buildings compared favorably with any in the world.

It was to the people of this city that St. Patrick's Cathedral opened its doors in May 1879. John Cardinal McCloskey, who four years earlier, had been the first American to be named a Cardinal, celebrated the Mass. Archbishop John Hughes, who first dreamed of this Cathedral, had died in the course of the twenty-one years of construction. It was Archbishop Hughes who disagreed with those who thought that the building site, "Hughes Folly," was too far uptown and felt strongly that one day it would be, in his words, "right in the center of the City."

Archbishop Hughes had deep convictions and vivid dreams. He insisted that his people receive fair and equal treatment in their Country and their City. He was equally insistent that they accept, to the full, their duties and responsibilities to the United States and to New York. He dreamed of the new Cathedral as part of the vitality of this City and as a House of God in which his people would find joy and deep pride. His prayer for St. Patrick's, that this Cathedral "may always be worthy of God, worthy of the Catholic religion, and an honor to this great City" is echoed here each day.

For one hundred years the Cathedral has fulfilled that prayer. Through all of these hectic years, she has watched as New York grew up around her to create the world's most famous skyline. She has seen millions come by land and sea and air to seek their fortune here and live out their lives. She has stretched out loving arms to welcome every race and class and culture.

I think Archbishop Hughes would be happy with St. Patrick's Cathedral in 1979. He was the first to have the dream and this Cathedral will always be, in a special sense, his. We are grateful to God that his dream lives on. In each generation, the Archbishop of New York, together with his priests, religious and faithful people, has dreamed of the spiritual mission of St. Patrick's and worked to build what was necessary for that mission. I can think of each of my predecessors and point to what was done in his time to continue the dream and enhance the mission. The Cathedral spires rose during the time of Cardinal McCloskey. The Lady Chapel came into existence because of the planning and perseverance of Archbishop Corrigan and Cardinal Farley. The years of the ministry of Cardinal Hayes were marked by the further enhancement of the interior of the Cathedral, and what a hugh debt of gratitude we owe to Francis Cardinal Spellman whose devotion to this Catheral is only hinted at by the beauty of the bronze doors and the grandeur of the altar and sanctuary.

What a presence this Cathedral is in our City! What an adornment of religion she has been for all her years.

While we sing the praises of the past, we come to envision the dream and the mission of the future. The towers of this Cathedral reaching to the sky challenge us to lift up our hearts to the Lord and give Him the best that is in us. In the days ahead we must, by the grace of God and the inspiration of His Holy Spirit, insure that the Church is alive and well in the service of mankind. We must call forth every gift bestowed upon the

Church. Everyone's human gift must be used, none may lay dormant, no talent left buried in the ground.

All of us, lay men and women, priests, religious, bishops; the young and old, the married and the single, the rich and poor; people of every race and tongue and culture, all the vast and beautiful variety that makes up the great Church of New York, all of us together have our work laid out for us as we move toward the twenty-first century. It is the work of spiritual renewal, of ever becoming a Church that will love God more ardently and be ready at the service of the modern world, with and under the leadership of our Holy Father, Pope John Paul II.

People love St. Patrick's for a variety of reasons. For many, love begins with the fascination of the Cathedral building itself. It is a pleasure that is almost unending as the allure of beautiful artifacts leads to a desire to know their history and understand their motivation. This is no small part of the Cathedral's mission, to free us from the stress of crises and bring us fuller perspectives.

I feel sure that all who read Leland Cook's history will come to know the warm reality of St. Patrick's. It is a sensitive, well documented, directly told story that will appeal to people who have known St. Patrick's for a life time as well as those approaching the Cathedral for the first time. I trust that its charming presentation of St. Patrick's will bring joy to many readers.

Introduction

by Brendan Gill

*I*n the Old World for well over a thousand years the center of a city was thought to be wherever its cathedral stood. The palace of a king might be grander, but it was universally considered to be of less importance than the house of God. If a king sat on a throne, so did a bishop, the appointed vicar of Christ, and Christianity taught that the bishop's throne, from which the cathedral took its name, was higher than that of any monarch.

At the heart of every great city in Europe—Rome, Paris, London, Vienna, Warsaw, Moscow—rises a cathedral, to which throughout history the inhabitants of the city have been drawn in times of trouble or rejoicing. Even in the case of towns and villages that lack a cathedral, one rightly assumes that a spire glimpsed from a long way off will lead one into an open space in front of a church and that this open space will prove to be the hub about which much of the life of the community revolves. (The old word for such a space is *parvis*, taken from the Latin word for Paradise.) What had been true for the Old World was true for the New World as well, in the early days after its discovery; by immemorial tradition, in the laying out of cities the deputies of God took precedence over the temporal ruler and his representatives.

That tradition was easy enough to follow in countries where religion and the governance of the state coincided and reinforced one another, as they did, for example, in South America. A different situation arose in North America after the Revolution and the founding of the United States. Henceforth, the separation of church and state would be absolute; instead of being subject to an official religion, every citizen was entitled to a free choice of religious beliefs and practices. At the time, the common religion of the country was Protestantism, an uneasy composite of innumerable differing sects. Congregationalists, Episcopalians, Presbyterians, Baptists, and the like, they were —such is the loving kindness of devout Christians!—at daggers drawn over the question of which sect among them was the inheritor of the true church of Christ. Their rivalry expressed itself in architectural as well as theological terms. No longer was there a single house of worship in a given community, serving as its center; on the contrary; there were many houses of worship and they competed as fiercely for favored sites as they did for social prestige and money.

In that fragmented and disputatious world of Protestantism, a few beliefs were capable of being shared; one of them was that wherever the truth of Christianity might lie, it was surely far from the errors and superstitions of Rome. In the early days of the Republic, Roman Catholics made up so small a portion of the population that they were looked upon as a curious aberration, not unlike the Jews, but when the great waves of immigration started crossing the Atlantic in the early decades of the nineteenth century, at first from Ireland and then from Germany, Italy, and Poland, a strong prejudice sprang up against Catholics. They were seen to be outsiders, incapable by temperament and religion of ever being successfully woven into the fabric of American life. As outsiders, they amounted to a danger; the most prudent way to deal with them was to make sure that they remained where they had found themselves on landing: isolated, impoverished, and despised.

It is against this background that we ought to judge the fantastic daring of John Hughes, fourth bishop and first archbishop of New York, when in 1850 he announced his intention of building a great new cathedral on Fifth Avenue between Fiftieth and Fifty-first streets. The site was a superb one, at the top of a low hill, with the land falling away on all four sides; it was also an entire block on what was rapidly becoming the most fashionable avenue in the city. If Hughes's "folly," as it soon came to be called, were ever to achieve reality, it would be by far the most impressive man-made object for many miles around. Moreover, Hughes's daring consisted not only in proposing so vast and costly an undertaking but also in perceiving that the cathedral could become, like the cathedrals of old, a central point in the future life of New York. From the start, he promised that it would be "worthy of God, worthy of the Catholic religion, and an honor to this great city." An honor? What on earth was happening to Protestant New York when it found itself being proffered honors based on Catholic piety and Catholic pennies? The city did well to gasp and shake its head. For what Hughes was indirectly announcing when he announced the building of a new cathdral was that the Catholics of New York were no longer to be thought of as outsiders; they were an integral part of the city's greatness and it was time that they took their rightful place in the community.

During the 1850s, the "folly" grew ever more ambitious in concept. The plans for it were being drawn by James Renwick, the most prominent architect in the city. Astonishingly, they revealed that the cathedral would be one of the biggest in all Christendom, constructed largely of marble, with a length on the exterior of over three hundred feet and with spires reaching over three hundred feet into the sky. The cornerstone was laid by Archbishop Hughes in 1858, before a record-breaking crowd of onlookers, and the cathedral was formally opened for worship in May 1879. Hughes had been dead for fifteen years by then, but he had seen ample evidence that his "folly" would flourish and that, given the location and immense scale of the cathedral, its importance to the city was bound to increase with time. He and Renwick had taken the boldest possible chances; ironically, to unthinking later generations they would give the impression of having been merely wise.

We are a city that, even within its comparatively narrow confines, has always tended to spin apart. To speak only of Manhattan (the original New York City of Hughes's day), we have Wall Street and Greenwich Village and Chinatown and Chelsea and Times Square and the Upper East Side and Riverside Drive and Harlem and Washington Heights and scores of other districts and neighborhoods; yet we have few places that convey an authentic sense of being at the very heart of things. St. Patrick's is such a place. Aided by the graceful presence of its neighbor, Rockefeller Center (and despite the impertinent overbearingness of another neighbor, the Olympic Tower), the cathedral dominates Fifth Avenue as easily today as it has ever done. Thanks to the program of preservation carried out under the watchful eye of Cardinal Cooke, the building has never looked more beautiful. There it stands for our delight and, if necessary, for our consolation. Its front steps are assuredly a parvis, if not a Paradise, and young and old take the sun upon their faces there as a sort of benediction, while the scattered benedictions of a thousand rosy candles wink and twinkle within. High above the green roof of the Lady chapel is a newly sculpted statue of the Virgin Mary. She smiles down upon us as we hurry past and that, too, is a benediction, for in her presence everything we look upon is blest.

Chapter 1: Old New York

Overleaf: Detail from a window of the Lady chapel. St. Isaac Jogues, the first priest to celebrate Mass in Manhattan, tortured and later murdered by Indians in 1646. The figure of St. Jogues is shown with mutilated right hand.

St. Patrick's Cathedral was called "Hughes' Folly" when construction started over 120 years ago, a comment on Archbishop John Hughes' decision to locate the church on the rural outskirts of the city. Building it cost twice as much and took four times as long as estimates had predicted, and some critics didn't like it when it was finished. The largest Roman Catholic cathedral in the United States has, however, become firmly established over the past century as a magnetic attraction for visitors, a beloved neighborhood church to thousands of New Yorkers, a building of immense dignity and spectacular beauty, a landmark worthy of the name. Its development over the years echoes and reflects that of its home city.

The Downtown Population Center

New York of 100 and more years ago was a thriving port. The excellent harbor afforded space and shelter for the frail craft of the eighteenth and nineteenth centuries, and the city-building started quite naturally at the harbor's edge. Freed from Dutch and British proprietorship, the "new" Americans devoted their energies to making lives and fortunes in a land the boundaries of which were barely defined. New York became the first port of call for those unhappy or adventurous enough to leave Europe, and westward expansion was well underway.

In what is now New York's financial center, the narrow tip of Manhattan Island was studded with wharves and docking facilities. Necessary warehouses formed a second waterside perimeter, and ancillary businesses — chandlers, lawyers, customs agents, exporters, taverns — fleshed out the bustling port. The city grew at an incredible pace, and, with water boundaries on all sides, the growth pattern had to be northward on Manhattan Island. Yet Manhattan north of the harbor was considered so untamed that when the present City Hall was constructed in 1803, the front, which pointed south and toward the city proper, was faced with marble whereas the back of the building, which faced north and would thus never be seen, was constructed of cheaper and æsthetically less pleasing red sandstone. Trinity Church's decision in 1807 to build St. John's Chapel in the outlying Varick Street caused irate parishioners to feel the new church to be better suited to missionary work, since its site was well beyond civilization. A donation of four acres of land at Broadway and Canal streets was refused by New York's Lutheran Society because it was not worth fencing. Canal Street, so named because of a drainage canal dug parallel to a large and scenic pond situated there in 1809, was at one time considered for a public park area, but the proposal was never seriously entertained, since New Yorkers would not travel to such a remote part of the city.

But by 1810, the northward growth pattern was established and the city fathers began a street plan for Manhattan. Surveyors braved farmers and land-owners who did not take kindly to seeing their property sliced up into square blocks and who chose methods available only to those with access to ferocious dogs and rotten vegetables to discourage the survey team.

The War of 1812 and the opening of the Erie Canal brought further growth to New York. The furs and richness of America's West poured into New York as the terminus of the canal, the forerunner of the then-unknown railroad. Commercial activity meant wealth, and in time the nabobs of the city began building splendid houses for themselves. By 1825, Peter Cooper's general store at the junction of Third and Fourth avenues marked the northern limits of the city. There farmers from nearer Greenwich village and the more distant Chelsea village would trade produce for Mr. Cooper's wares. A decade later, New York's Potter's Field was to be converted into the fashionable Washington Square and ringed with houses belonging to some of New York's first families.

The rapidly changing outskirts of the city were generally populated by squatters and shanty-dwellers who lived as best they could. One squalid settlement after another was transformed as the city moved uptown. Union Square was a ragged assortment of makeshift dwellings and unkempt fields, but by 1845 this section was the most prestigious address in town.

New York was a logical choice for the capital city of the newly formed United States of America, and it undoubtedly would have been so designated had it not been for congressional insistence that the nation's capital be territorially ceded to the federal government. New Yorkers even then were not about to trade away a boundless prosperity for prestige, and President Washington, after some desultory excursions to examine the unsettled and then-remote Long Island as a compromise site, ultimately chose his own Potomac area for America's federal city.

Religious New York

Church growth kept pace with the sprawling city, and the homogeneous quality of the population meant a comparable mix of houses of worship. As early as 1628, Reverend Jonas Michaelius, newly arrived from Holland, organized a congregation which worshipped in the loft of a stable. Peter Minuit served as one of the elders. In 1633 the first formal New York City church—a small wooden structure on Broad Street—was built by the Dutch. A second Dutch missionary, the Reverend Evarardus Bogardus, accompanied by a schoolteacher, Adam Rollandsen, arrived in the same year, and these two opened the first church school in the colonies. Within the earthworks of Fort Amsterdam, a three-sided citadel on the site of what is now Bowling Green, a small stone church was dedicated in 1642. It was called St. Nicholas in honor of the patron saint of Manhattan, and it was at this church that the Dutch worshipped for the next fifty years.

As the city prospered, and the need for fortification became less immediate, churches were constructed outside the walls of the fort. In 1693, a Dutch church was built on Exchange Place (then called Garden Street), and in 1729 the Old Middle Church was dedicated on Nassau Street. A third, called the North Church because of its uptown location, was built in 1769 in Williams Street, and these three churches served the members of the Collegiate Reformed Protestant Dutch Church.

The small church within Fort Amsterdam was no longer Dutch Reformed. The British fleet arrived in 1664, seized the fort, and appropriated St. Nicholas for services of the Church of England. St. Nicholas was used for the next thirty years, until March 1697, when a small wooden building was dedicated on the site of the present Trinity Church at the head of Wall Street. This church, also called Trinity, served as a meeting place for New York's Episcopalians for over forty years. The original building was destroyed by fire in 1776, rebuilt in 1788. Today's Trinity Church was built on the same site in 1846.

The American Revolution put this church in singular disfavor since its members were pledged to the service of the English king and parliament. But the elimination of blatantly British rituals, which included prayers for the king, and the consecration of American-born bishops paved the way for the American homogenization of what was to become the most powerful Protestant denomination in New York. With an endowment based on ownership of the Queen's Farm—a large tract of land from Christopher to Vesey streets—the Protestant Episcopal Church is one of New York's richest landlords, owning a sizable section of the downtown city.

The Lutherans were the next denomination to appear in New York, although gaining a toehold in the New World was to be difficult for this German-based church. Governor Peter Stuyvesant in 1653 forbade public assembly at any service except the Dutch Reformed. This proclamation was the first, but not the last, colonial mandate against freedom of religious choice. It was simply common sense to the ruling faction to prohibit public meetings sponsored by those not in power. Consequently, the Duth forbade religious services not Dutch, the British forbade worship outside the Episcopal Church, and so on down the ages. Stuyvesant's patrons, the Dutch West India Company, chided him for his intolerance, but Lutherans were not granted formal recognition until 1664 under the aegis of an English governor, Richard Nicholls.

This recognition was short lived, and when the Dutch reclaimed possession of Manhattan in 1674, they ordered the only Lutheran church in New York demolished as an obstacle to defense in case of attack. Another piece of land, however, was given in recompense and four square rods "between the city wall and the property of George Cobbett"[1] (Broadway and Rector Street) was deeded to the church. The fact that the Dutch influence in New York was strong enough to determine the language of church services offended the German-speaking majority of the congregation, and a schism developed between the two factions. The Lutheran German Christ Church started its own meetings at an abandoned brewery, but ultimately rejoined their Dutch brethren in 1789 when it became obvious that English would be America's mother tongue. The Germans had the last word in 1866, when an act of legislature officially dubbed the church the German Evangelical Lutheran Church of Saint Matthew.

One of New York's largest sects, the Presbyterian, began services in 1706. Out of favor with the authorities, this Scottish religious group had no formal church and met in sympathetic private houses. Reverend Francis McKemie was actually imprisoned for baptizing a child in 1707, but by 1719 a Presbyterian church — the forerunner of today's First Presbyterian Church — was opened on Wall Street. This single building served New York's Presbyterians until 1809.

The "total immersion" rite of the Baptists and the paranoia of the times made establishment of this sect as difficult as any in the New World. In 1709, a Baptist minister, William Wickenden, was imprisoned for three months for preaching without specific permission from the authorities, and the first formal church founded in 1712 was defunct by 1720. In 1745, services were once again held in a loft on William Street, and a small stone church was built in 1760. The post-revolutionary times proved especially hard for this sect, with its congregation scattered by the war, but a larger church was built in 1802 and the Baptist Church became solidly established in New York.

Relative latecomers to these shores, the Methodists arrived in 1766, soon after the sect showed strength in England. Early services were held in what was probably the same loft used by the Baptists, who had moved on to their own church, but by 1768 the Methodists had built Wesley Chapel in John Street. The rigid laws regarding public services in nonestablishment churches still prevailed, so the Methodist chapel, which was built as a house, was finished in the interior to qualify it as a private dwelling. It had a fireplace and chimney and was, therefore, legally a house, not a church. This technicality, which meant that parishioners had to use ladders to get to the upper galleries, gave New York Methodists a place in the new America.

There were also Jews in early New York, and this intrepid religion, inured to centuries of persecution in Europe, found the New World comparatively

This view of Battery Place was taken in 1853 and is one of the earliest outdoor photos of the city. The steeple of Trinity Church can be seen at right and, in the distance, the steeple of St. Paul's Chapel appears just above the rooflines.

easy. In 1695 there were twenty Jewish families in New York, but no place of worship was approved until 1729, when the first synagogue was opened at Mill and Beaver streets. This temple served the Spanish and Portuguese Jews who had moved to New York from Rhode Island. The swelling numbers of immigrants added to the New York City Jewish population, and a century later there were forty-seven temples, synagogues, and charitable institutions, all stoutly supported by the city's Jewish community.

Catholics in New York

The Roman Catholic Church in New York faced particular hardship because of the British rule. The struggle between England and Ireland resulted in extraordinary laws designed to suppress the Irish, for whom the Catholic religion was so much a fact of life that Irish nationality automatically meant Catholicism. These oppressive laws were transmitted to the New World as well, and New York's early lawgivers provided death by hanging to any Roman Catholic priest who might enter the city of his own free will. In 1643, before Father Isaac Jogues, a Jesuit missionary who had been tortured by the Mohawk Indians, sailed back to France, he heard the confessions of two people; we can assume there were at least that many devout Catholics in America at that time. Other Jesuits followed Jogues, but spread of the religion was severely hampered by the strict anti-Catholic laws. In 1741,

a man was actually hanged as a suspected Catholic priest, but he was also considered a fomenter of the Negro riot of that year.

Battery Park today.

The accession of James II to the English throne and his appointment, in 1682, of the Catholic Thomas Dongan as New York's governor paved the way for the establishment of the first Catholic congregation in 1785. The first priest to tend his flock in New York with official approval was the Reverend Ferdinand Farmer, a German Jesuit who had sporadically ministered to the thin population of New York Catholics from his home base in Pennsylvania. With the ouster of British rule, French and Spanish diplomats sympathetic to the Catholic cause strongly suggested to the new United States governors that Catholicism be openly allowed. There were at that time between twenty and two hundred Catholics in New York.

It is interesting, and perhaps important, to note at this point that Catholics in America took their lead from existing and better-known Protestant church techniques. Trustees, respected men of the community, were responsible for the functioning of the Church. Priests were there to service the congregation spiritually, and to deliver—if they were good—sermons of sufficient vigor and persuasion to guarantee a weekly revenue from parishioners. The trustees approved all expenses, including the priest's stipends, and were responsible for Church debts and internal management. The first Catholic church—to be called St. Peter's—was created under the trustee system and with the help of a $1,000 gift from King Charles of Spain (the king of France, Louis XVI, with a

St. Frances X. Cabrini (below) and Venerable Kateri Tekakwitha (right) two figures from the great bronze doors at the main entrance of St. Patrick's. In all, twenty-one figures by the English sculptor John Angel adorn the doors designed by Charles D. Maginnis.

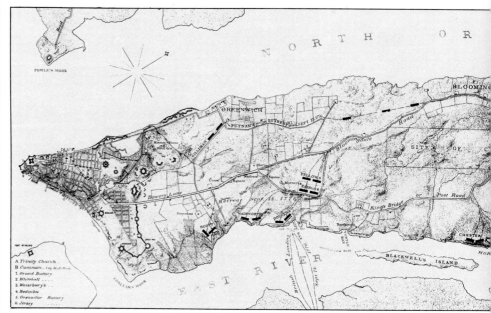

revolution at his doorstep, did not respond to the American plea for aid).

A parcel of five lots was obtained from five leaseholders to the Episcopalian Trinity Church, and a subsequent petition requesting outright purchase of the plot resulted in the acquisition of the site of St. Peter's on Barclay and Church streets, then still the outskirts of the young New York. Coincidentally, this was the place at which John Ury was executed as a Catholic priest in 1741. The cornerstone of the first Roman Catholic Church in New York was laid in 1785 at a ceremony presided over by the Spanish minister and other distinguished citizens.

St. Peter's first pastor was Charles Whelan, a zealous, well-educated Capuchin priest who seemed incapable of delivering the bombastic rhetoric common among "good" preachers of the day. The congregation did not like Reverend Whelan, and when Andrew Nugent was appointed assistant pastor, loyalty quickly swung to the newer man. The trustees, acting with the support of the parishioners, moved to remove Father Whelan, first by denying him any living expenses. At that time Catholic trustees, it should be recalled, had the legal and ecclesiastical right to choose and depose their pastors. The American Catholic Church was as yet such an unformed association that European precedents did not necessarily apply, and often strong personalities and political exigencies determined church administrative practices. Father Whelan was finally forced out before the completion of St. Peter's. The triumphant Father Nugent was apparently so flushed with his victory that he demanded a $400 annual salary, as opposed to the $300 offered by the trustees of St. Peter's. They told him to take it or leave it, and he took it, singing the first mass in St. Peter's on 4 November 1786, approximately one year after the cornerstone had been laid.

His victory was short lived. The combustible mixture of Irish, French, German, Italian, Spanish, Scots, and English parishioners soon found fault with the combative Father Nugent. He, however, was less docile than his predecessor, and some stormy sessions ensued. Ultimately Father Nugent was

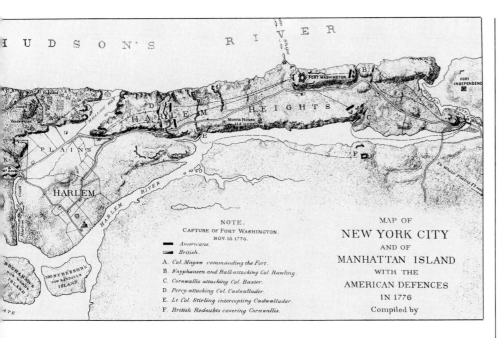

removed by the trustees, who were still following Protestant principles regarding the relations between a pastor and his congregation and the temporal administration of church affairs.

St. Peter's survived its early growing pains, largely through subsidy from Catholics in Spain and Mexico, who were shamelessly and repeatedly asked for aid, but by the early nineteenth century the increasing Catholic population found the church structure inadequate. Church reorganization had turned New York into an Episcopal See, which meant a resident bishop for the community. A bishop had to have a proper cathedral, and the faithful were determined to welcome their prestigious cleric with a suitable edifice.

In 1808, Canal Street was New York's northern boundary, running through suburban villas of the wealthy die-hard farmers and the shanties of squatters. The new cathedral was to be built between Broadway and the Bowery, the two main thoroughfares of the city, just north of the Collect, the large pond and surroundings once deemed too remote for a city park. Even then, the land was wild enough "that foxes were frequent visitors."[2]

The War of 1812 checked immigration to America and worked economic hardships on the country, with the result that work on the new cathedral was severely inhibited. Nonetheless, a Jesuit boys' school started in a rented house across the street from the site of the yet-to-be-built cathedral proved a great success and, with an eye toward the future, the trustees of St. Peter's, who were nominally administering the affairs of the new cathedral, bought two blocks of land uptown on the pioneering Madison Avenue. The school was relocated there for a time, but was so far uptown that it did not prosper and shortly closed. The land, however, remained as part of St. Peter's.

Work on the new building continued, and, to the surprise and pleasure of Catholics and non-Catholics alike, the finished product was an architectural jewel. At a time when building *per se* was a matter of utility and when the only edifice of aesthetic pretensions was the Episcopal Trinity Church, the new Catholic cathedral made all New Yorkers quietly proud.

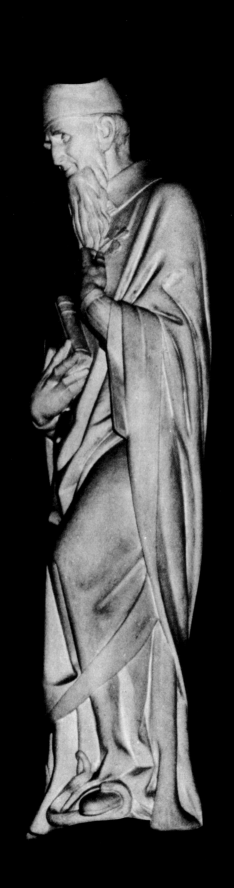

Chapter 2:
The Church

The Church, the Trustees, and John Hughes

New York's first bishop—actually its second, since the Irish Bishop Concanon died before he could see his new diocese—Bishop Connally arrived from Dublin after an Atlantic crossing of sixty-eight days. He took possession of the new church the day he arrived, 15 May 1815. The cathedral was designated St. Patrick's, after Ireland's patron saint, and from its dedication a honeymoon period began between parishioners, trustees, and Church hierarchy. The diocese of New York had only three churches, two in New York and one in Albany, to accommodate 13,000 Catholics, and St. Patrick's on Mott Street became the center. A Catholic orphanage was founded under the auspices of St. Elizabeth Seton's Sisters of Charity; a parochial school was established in the basement of the cathedral; adult education classes for immigrants were begun throughout the city; and Catholicism was solidly established in New York.

Expansion inevitably brought problems, and the old trustee system once more faced them. St. Peter's trustees were reluctant to oversee the responsibility of two churches. Consequently, St. Patrick's formed its own board of trustees, independent of the senior St. Peter's and totally responsible for all but the "spiritual affairs" of the cathedral. Upon the death of Bishop Connally, John DuBois was named bishop of St. Patrick's in 1826. The trustees were not pleased. They flexed their financial muscles regarding his salary and that of his rector, and the relationship deteriorated rapidly. DuBois, beset by age and physical ailments as well as the demands of a testy board of trustees, was too frail for the daily problems of a fast-growing parish. A co-adjutor to St. Patrick's was named in 1835. The post was actually a clerical administrative one, designed to relieve a sickly or overworked prelate from much of the daily routine. The man chosen for the job was to prove one of the most influential men in New York.

The Reverend John Hughes was an Irishman who arrived in Baltimore in 1817. Because of the stern anti-Catholic laws then in force in Ireland, Hughes

OLD ST. PATRICK'S CATHEDRAL, MOTT ST.
1808.

PHOTOGRAVURE & COLOR CO. N.Y.

Old St. Patrick's Cathedral in flames, as sketched on 20 October 1866, the morning after the fire. (Right) The cathedral was rebuilt in 1868.

was an uneducated twenty-year-old determined to become a priest. He was ordained in 1825 in Philadelphia, and soon made a name for himself as a flamboyant and controversial figure in the Church. An instinctive orator, he was popular with Catholics and non-Catholics alike. In a squabble with his trustees, he simply set about building a new church without trustees. His presence made the new church a fashionable one, and the truculent trustees found themselves administering to a church without a congregation.

Hughes was also an articulate spokesman against the then-prevalent anti-Catholic sentiment. He once acted as anonymous "stringer" for *The Protestant*, an anti-Papacy publication that specialized in scandalous stories about priests and nuns. Hughes fed this periodical totally fictitious stories that were printed *in toto* without any attempt at verification. His subsequent public exposure of the magazine's irresponsibility gained for him further popularity with the public even as it earned him ecclesiastical censure for his stunt.

But his reputation was forever made in a series of debates with Dr. John Breckinridge, a Presbyterian minister with little sympathy for the Catholic Church or its members. The meetings between the suave, aristocratic Breckinridge and the eloquent and theatrical Reverend Hughes became popular entertainment of the day, and Philadelphia citizens, regardless of creed, cheered Reverend Hughes as he systematically destroyed his opponent. With a gregarious nature and sometimes cutting wit, John Hughes gave a new dimension to the stereotyped image of the clergy. Such a dynamic man was destined for ecclesiastical success. The troubles in the growing New York diocese beckoned to Hughes in 1838. Bishop DuBois at that time was in very frail health and his trustees completely dominated him. The churches of New York City were deeply in debt and the congregations openly split between affiliation with their bishop and with the trustees. Priests were often insubordinate to the bishop if they were supported by the trustees, and Catholic morale in the city was at low ebb.

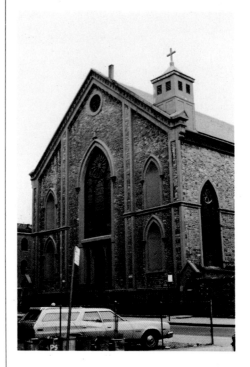

Hughes knew his own strengths. He called a meeting of St. Patrick's pew-holders, and his pulpit style did not fail him. Equating the trustees to the villainous perpetrators of the English penal laws in Ireland, he asked if Catholics would pledge their loyalty to their church or to those who would once again persecute her. The congregation (mostly Irish, it should be noted) unanimously backed the new Bishop Hughes, and the bewildered trustees found themselves ousted. Hughes reported to a Philadelphia friend: "We have brought the trustees so low that they are not able to give even a decent kick."[1]

Taming the trustees was only the first step in Bishop Hughes' career in New York. Mindful of his own lack of education, he set about establishing parochial schools and seminaries throughout the diocese. To relieve the immense church debt, he traveled to Europe to seek funds from the wealthy and tried to establish a common church fund, which would help the parishes in the greatest financial danger. St. Peter's, the first church in the city, was actually bankrupt, so mismanaged by its trustees that it was ordered sold to pay its notes. Hughes asked for and was granted assignment of the debt from the Court of Appeals and took title to the St. Peter's property, which at that time included those uptown lots on Fifth Avenue.

Chapter 3:
The Site

How the Church Came to Own the Land

In the late 1890s, a number of years after St. Patrick's Cathedral had been opened for worship, a framed paper entitled "Abstract to the Cathedral Property" appeared in the vestibule of each side entrance. It listed the various real estate changes through which the Fifth Avenue plot had passed over the past century or so, and described when and how the church came into its possession. It was still there some years later, around the time the cathedral was consecrated in 1910, when the rector's office explained to newspapers that this somewhat unusual display of the title history had been put up "to interest the public" and as a "matter of general information in view of the many inquiries constantly made regarding the acquirement of the property for general purposes."[1]

The public, especially in the years since property values along that stretch of Fifth Avenue had escalated wildly, had, in fact, often been outspokenly curious about just how the Catholic Church happened to own this choice piece of land. A common assumption held that Catholic authorities had, in return for votes, persuaded the city to give them the land for one dollar, or, perhaps, a lease at one dollar a year for 999 years. In 1882, William L. Stone, editor of the well-respected *New York Journal of Commerce*, printed an article on the land title to clear up "a very common impression that the property was acquired without due consideration," an impression he felt was "circulated by persons who are prejudiced against the present owners."[2] Again, in 1893, an exhaustive study on the subject was made, but twelve years after that, Charles Hemstreet, in a book called *Nooks and Corners of Old New York*, was furthering the rumor: "At Fiftieth Street and Fifth Avenue is St. Patrick's Cathedral, the corner-stone of which was laid in 1858. The entire block on which it stands was, the preceding year, given to the Roman Catholics for a nominal sum—one dollar—by the city."[3]

The 1893 examination of the cathedral's claim to the property was con-

(Right) Cartoon of the archbishop carrying a miniature of the cathedral with its deed tucked under his arm, a reference to the false information given out that the Catholic Church had obtained the property at a very low price (*Harper's Magazine*, March 1873).

A NEW READING OF AN OLD PARABLE.

ducted by a lawyer, and later Supreme Court judge, Henry R. Beekman. His findings, he wrote, did not support "a feeling on the part of many that an indefensible use has been made of the public property."[4] The results of his study were summarized, starting in 1796, when

...Casimir T. Goerck laid out what were known as the common lands belonging to the Mayor, Aldermen, and Commonalty of the city of New York into blocks bounded on the north and south by unnamed streets, sixty feet in width. The property in question forms a part of Block No. 62 on said map, which in 1799 was conveyed by the Mayor, Aldermen, and Commonalty of the city of New York to one Robert Lylburn for the sum of £405 and a perpetual quit rent of "four bushels of good merchantable wheat or the value thereof in gold or silver coin of lawful money of the State of New York, payable on May 1st of each and every year".... The property was conveyed by Lylburn in 1810 to Francis Thompson and Thomas Cadle, who in turn sold it to Andrew Morris and Cornelius Heeney (Church officials), by whom it was mortgaged in 1810 to the Eagle Fire Company of New York, and in 1821 conveyed to one Dennis Doyle, subject to said mortgage.[5]

Francis Cooper then purchased the land at public auction in 1828 and on 30 January 1829, as recorded in the Register's Office,

conveyed the same property to the trustees of St. Peter's Church in the City of New York. The recitals in this deed state that just prior to the sale in the foreclosure proceedings, Francis Cooper, Peter Duffy, Cornelius Heeney, Garret Byrne, and Hugh Sweeney, acting on behalf of the trustees of St. Patrick's Cathedral and St. Peter's Church, had selected the property in question for a burial-ground, and had designated Francis Cooper to attend the sale and bid for the property; that the purchase was accordingly made by Cooper for $5,550, which money, as well as an additional sum of $51.53, exacted by the master of Chancery for interest, was paid in equal parts by the trustees of St. Patrick's Cathedral and the trustees of St. Peter's Church, and that the property was purchased by Cooper and the title thereto taken by him for these two corporations which had advanced the purchase money.... Thus the title to the property became vested in these two bodies by purchase at public auction for a substantial consideration, and some thirty years after the city of New York had parted with its title.[6]

In 1811, the city adopted a new plan of streets and avenues, which, as it turned out much later, put St. Patrick's Cathedral in possession of a small, irregular strip running along the north side of Fifty-first Street between Fifth Avenue and what was then Fourth Avenue, at the southern border of a city-owned block, and left the city with a roughly comparable strip along the north side of Fiftieth Street, the southern boundary of the cathedral. In 1852, the city and the Church exchanged their mutually inconvenient strips, an agreement that was "in pursuance of a general plan and in no respect different from a large number of other cases of a like character."[7]

Two other changes regarding the property took place that year, one a transaction that had become routine as the city moved farther away from its rural roots, the other a significant development in the history of the Church in New York. Ever since the original grant to Robert Lylburn, the owners of the Fiftieth Street plot had continued to pay to the city the quitrent of four bushels of wheat or their equivalent in current money, these rents being "perpetual in the character"[8] of such property grants. But this kind of bookkeeping had become too cumbersome to a government increasingly involved in land subdivisions and sales, and the city adopted the policy of translating these rather quaint fees into one lump sum and discontinuing future annual payments. St. Patrick's Cathedral's "four bushels of wheat" was decided to be worth $83.32, representing the current value of a bushel of wheat at $1.25 and including a capitalization at 6 percent. The sum was paid to the city by the trustees and so recorded in the Register's Office on 11 November 1852.

Around the same time, reports Mr. Beekman's study, "the trustees of St. Peter's Church conveyed their interest to the trustees of St. Patrick's Cathedral, who thus became sole owners of the property."[9] The Cathedral explained later that the St. Peter's shares had been "sold" at public auction to the trustees of St. Patrick's for the sum of $59,500. The transaction gives a fair reflection of the state of finances of St. Peter's at the time and of the efforts of John Hughes. (Bishop Hughes had been named Archbishop of the newly created Archdiocese of New York in 1850.)

Mr. Beekman finished his report with the opinion that in all these matters "the dealings of the city with the Cathedral differed in no wise from a large number of similar ones had by the city with other owners of portions of its common lands, and it is apparent upon the face of the facts as I have detailed them, that the criticisms which have been passed upon the method of acquisition by the Cathedral of its property are wholly without foundation or justification."[10] It is true that lands were leased by the city gratuitously or for nominal considerations to charitable organizations, and that in this category was the property occupied for some time by the Roman Catholic Orphan Asylum, just one block north of St. Patrick's.

Before the Cathedral

*I*t is highly unlikely that any of the church fathers involved in these early years with the plot of land "out of town" had any notion it could be put to grand purpose or would eventually be one of the most valuable pieces of real estate on Manhattan Island. Shortly after the original purchase in 1810, an old "mansion" on the property became the home of the New York Literary Institution, the Jesuit school for the sons of the best families, that had been started in a rented house opposite the cathedral on Mulberry Street. When the school closed about three years later, the building was taken over by the Trappist monks, who used it for an orphan asylum, another venture that ended shortly after its inception. (Until 1835, when St. Paul's Church was established at One hundred seventeenth Street, the old Jesuit school was the only place above downtown Manhattan where mass was celebrated. The same buildings were used as the rectory for the new Church of St. John the Evangelist in 1841, and later moved to the east side of Madison Avenue to make way for the new Cathedral.)

By the late 1820s, when the land came again to the attention of the

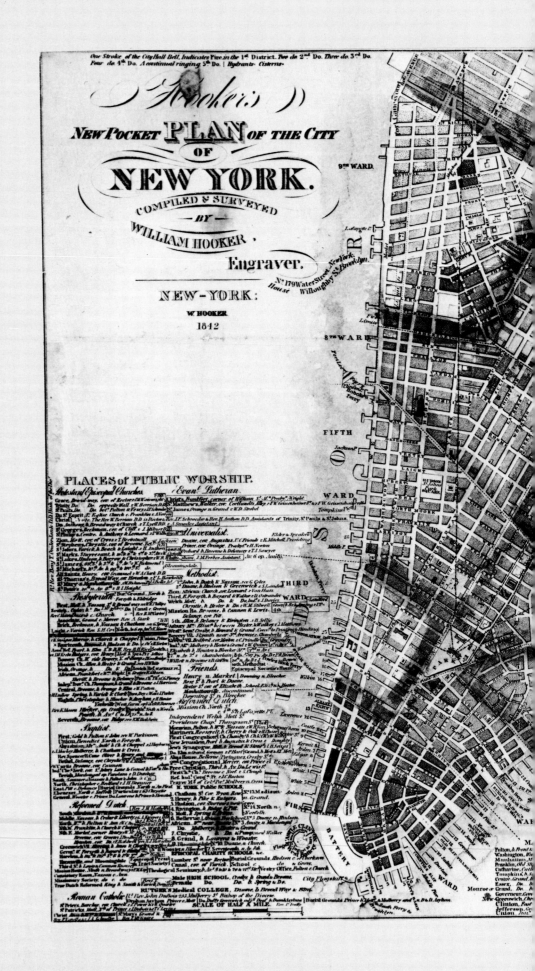

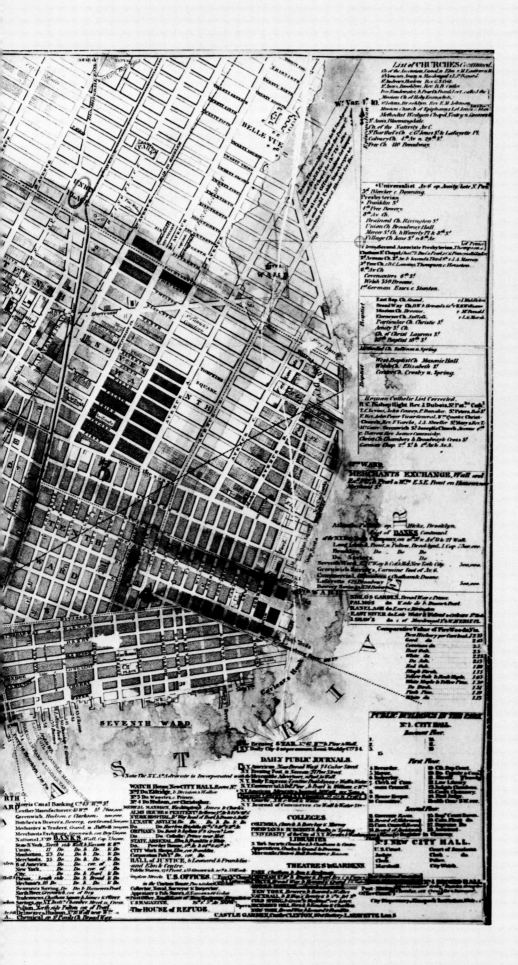

church trustees, it was as the possible site of a new cemetery. This was by no means a well-supported plan, though the need for a cemetery did exist. One interested party protested against the purchase of the land because it was four or five miles distant from City Hall and not suited for burial purposes. It was, in fact, too rocky, but the trustee committee appointed to examine the site did not do so and the purchase went ahead. Some records indicate that a burial vault was built on the premises in the 1830s, later to be closed along with the church's Eleventh Street cemetery.

Before Archibishop Hughes began to implement his dream of a great cathedral, no one paid much attention to the property, and with good reason. New York in the 1830s was a bustling place, but all the activity was still very much downtown, well below Thirty-fourth Street. Farther north were orchards, vegetable gardens, common lands of the city, a farmhouse or gentleman's country seat or summer residence here and there, and relatively isolated villages, such as Manhattanville way up on the Hudson River at about One hundred twenty-fifth Street. Fifth Avenue houses above Thirty-fourth Street were very definitely "suburban." One of them was the elaborate Gothic villa owned by William Coventry Waddell, complete with gardens, conservatory, and cottage lodge, at Thirty-eighth Street. A young girl described her visit to this home in 1849: "Fifth Avenue is very muddy above Eighteenth Street, and there are no blocks of houses as there are downtown, but only two or three on a block. Last Saturday we had a picnic on the grounds of Mr. Waddell's country seat way up Fifth Avenue and it was so muddy I spoiled my new light cloth gaiter boots."[11]

Manhattan's first railroad, the New York and Harlem, ran up Fourth Avenue and had been completed by 1834 as far north as Yorkville, well into the countryside. Although the city had set aside a large piece of land, starting at Fifth Avenue and Fifty-ninth Street on the east, and plans for Central Park were proposed by 1850, work on the area did not get underway until several years later, as part of a public works program intended to ease the unemployment problems created by the financial panic and depression of 1857. Before the work of clearing and planting the land began, following the design of·Frederick Law Olmsted and Calvert Vaux, Central Park was a rocky stretch of scrubby ground, described by one observer as "a bare, unsightly, and disgusting spot."[12] It and much of the surrounding area north of Forty-second Street was home to unpleasant taverns, garbage dumps, and shantytowns, which housed perhaps as many as 10,000 squatters and uncounted numbers of pigs, goats, and chickens. The most notorious of these shantytowns was "Dutch Hill," around Forty-second Street near the East River, composed, said the *Daily Tribune,* of shacks "built of slabs, old boards, timber from torn-down houses, old tin roofing rolled up and spread out again," the unhappy site of "poverty, misery, beggary, starvation, crimes, filth, and licentiousness."[13] They were, in fact, home to the hundreds of immigrant laborers who moved north as the city did, executing the hard work of leveling the ground and grading roads. The *New York Times* reported in July 1858:

There are 1,500 laborers employed at the Central Park at present, of whom 100 are grubbing, 100 draining, 150 with 75 carts removing dirt, and the rest making roads. Since the work on the park commenced, 287 houses and shanties have been removed from the grounds; thirteen acres of the skating-pond have been excavated; forty acres of land have been grubbed; sixty acres of the lower pond have been drained; sixty-third street has been leveled; considerable blasting has been done, and a great deal of rock removed, and a wall has been built around the entire Park. About five-sixths of the promenade is graded, and the drive for half a mile will be graded in a few weeks.[14]

A photograph of people skating in the unfinished Central Park a year later —taking part in "healthful amusement and recreation," as the Parks Commissioner's report stated —shows shacks still standing in the background along the stretch now occupied by the Plaza and other Fifty-ninth Street hotels.

Around the time construction on the park was getting underway, an area a little further south on Fifth Avenue was being considered by the trustees of Columbia College as the site of their new buildings. The plot, called in Columbia documents the "Upper Estate," ran almost to Sixth Avenue on the west and between Forty-seventh and Fifty-first streets, directly opposite what would become St. Patrick's Cathedral. The Upper Estate had already had an interesting history. Part of the common lands of the city, it had been acquired around 1804, for $5,000, by Dr. David Hosack, a professor of botany and medicine, the physician who ministered to the dying Alexander Hamilton after his duel with Aaron Burr, and one of the founders of the College of Physicians and Surgeons. He opened on the grounds the Elgin Botanical Gardens, a bucolic spot with a greenhouse, two hothouses, exotic trees and gardens, and medicinal plants, from the sale of which he hoped to make a profit. The gardens were enjoyed by the public and used as a teaching aid, but Dr. Hosack found it a financially draining enterprise and in 1810 sold it to the state, which in turn gave it to Columbia as its share of a state lottery run for "the promotion of literature and other purposes."[15] The college was expected to move to the plot within a set number of years and to maintain the botanical gardens in the meantime.

The trustees were less than excited by this grant of land. Although the college was eager to move to new quarters from its downtown schoolhouse, Fifth Avenue and Fifty-first Street did not offer an inviting surrounding. They delayed for years development of the property; in the 1830s Dr. Hosack's garden disappeared once and for all, and finally, in 1854, the architect Richard Upjohn was asked to design buildings for the site. But Columbia representatives who checked out the spot shortly after excavation work had begun found it forbidding, "a mile beyond civilization,"[16] dangerous to the health and morals of students, and, most important, completely undesirable for possible leasing to tenants. The cost of preparing and building on the land would be greater than anyone could justify after examining the site. The college decided two years later to occupy a spot just one block east, taking the cheaper alternative of moving into the already existing buildings of the New York

The Croton Reservoir as it was at the turn of the century. The New York Public

Institute for the Instruction of the Deaf and Dumb on Madison Avenue and Fiftieth Street. There they remained during the long years, and beyond, in which the Catholic cathedral slowly took form. Some authorities say that the decision to build St. Patrick's on the grounds of the church's would-be uptown cemetery was influenced in part by the pleasant prospect of facing Columbia College gardens directly across Fifth Avenue.

Churches and Churchgoers

The push uptown, however, as downtown areas were increasingly taken over by commercial interests, was steady and inevitable during the middle and later years of the century. Charitable and educational institutions and churches were the first to move north along Fifth Avenue and nearby. Scattered among the derelict areas and the occasional brownstone row houses were the Colored Orphan Asylum (sometimes called the Colored Home for the Aged and Indigent) between Forty-third and Forty-fourth streets, St. Luke's Hospital at Fifty-fourth, and the Institute for the Deaf and Dumb. The Dripps map of New York, officially named the "Map of the City

Library now stands on the Forty-second Street site.

of New York Extending Northward to Fiftieth Street," was drawn and published in 1851; a companion map printed later covered the area north of Fiftieth Street. The first published maps to include in detail every structure and lot in the city, these amazing drawings show the buildings surrounding St. Patrick's during the early years of its construction: Directly across Fifty-first Street was the Catholic Male Orphan Asylum, one block to the east was the Female Orphan Asylum. Immediately opposite the huge distributing reservoir of the aqueduct farther downtown was Rutgers Female College. And, religious groups of all denominations were finding Fifth Avenue north an increasingly hospitable neighborhood for their congregations and their splendid new churches. Emanu-el, a striking Moorish-style temple, was built at the corner of Fifth Avenue and Forty-third Street in the late 1860s. Mr. Waddell's sumptuous "country seat" was replaced in 1858 by the Brick Presbyterian Church. Somewhat later came the Collegiate Church of St. Nicholas at Forty-eighth Street, Fifth Avenue Presbyterian at Fifty-fifth Street, and the enormously wealthy St. Thomas' Episcopal Church at Fifty-third Street. There was a handsome white granite Dutch Reformed Church at Twenty-ninth Street, Christ Church Episcopal at Thirty-fifth Street, and the Church

(Right) Opposite the Croton Reservoir on Fifth Avenue stood the House of Mansions, a complex of residences erected in 1856. Temple Emanu-El can be seen just beyond in this 1875 photograph.

An 1894 photograph of Fifth Avenue showing the Fifth Avenue Collegiate Church at Forty-eighth Street.

of the Divine Paternity (Universalist) at Forty-fifth Street. Writing in 1872, James D. McCabe, Jr., in *Lights and Shadows of New York Life; or Sights and Sensations of the Great City*, made some mildly cranky observations on New Yorkers' Sunday habits:

Towards ten o'clock the streets begin to fill up with churchgoers. The cars are crowded, and handsome carriages dash by conveying their owners to their places of worship. The uptown churches are the most fashionable, and are the best attended, but all the sacred edifices are well filled on Sunday morning. New York compromises with its conscience by a scrupulous attendance upon morning worship, and reserves the rest of the day for its own convenience. The uptown churches all strive to get in, or as near as possible to, the

The Villard Houses, located behind the cathedral on Madison Avenue, at one time housed the offices of the archidiocese of New York.

Fifth avenue. One reason for this is, doubtless, the desire that all well-to-do New Yorkers have to participate in the after-church promenade. The churches close their services near about the same hour, and then each pours its throng of fashionably dressed people into the avenue. The congregations of distant churches all find their way to the avenue, and for about an hour after church the splendid street presents a very attractive spectacle.[17]

Mr. McCabe thought New Yorkers, despite the abundance of churches available to them, could "hardly be said to be a church-going people" and he was "astonished" to see "the widespread carelessness which prevails here on the subject of church-going."[18] Sunday afternoons were given over to enter-

(Opposite page) The Easter Parade on Fifth Avenue at the turn of the century. (Left) Engraving of Fifth Avenue viewed northward from Forty-second Street. The Moorish-styled Temple Emanu-El is at right. (Below) Looking north from Fifty-first Street showing the Vanderbilt residences at left and St. Thomas' Episcopal Church.

tainments — picnics, pleasure boating, the Bowery beer-gardens, concerts — and no one seemed to think it sinful to spend the Lord's Day at such pursuits. McCabe thought it was a sign of the times:

One reason for this dissipation is plain. People are so much engrossed in the pursuit of wealth that they really have no leisure time in the week. They must take Sunday for relaxation and recreation, and they grudge the few hours in the morning that decency requires them to pass in church. [19]

Residential Fifth Avenue

The pursuit of wealth, and the extraordinary success in that pursuit of a small number of people, was the factor that changed once and for all the area around St. Patrick's Cathedral from suburban wilderness to swell address. Alexander Turney Stewart's gargantuan home at Thirty-fourth Street, begun in 1869, set the style to come. Appleton's *New York Illustrated* wrote at the time that no building on the Avenue would

probably ever be so famous as the marble palace of Mr. A.T. Stewart.... This will unquestionably be when completed, the most costly and luxurious private residence on the continent. Even in its present unfinished state words are almost inadequate to describe the beauty and unique grandeur of some of the details of its construction. Mr. Stewart hopes to have it ready for occupation by next fall. Before he enters it as a tenant it will have cost him upward of two million dollars. [20]

Although Mr. Stewart and his wife lived in the house for only a little over fifteen years, and although the streets nearby were in his lifetime taken over by trade and commercial interests, his "marble palace" was the first of a series of splendid private mansions, one more elaborate and ostentatious than the next, built up along Fifth Avenue in the gravy years after the Civil War.

A few adventurous and farsighted individuals — and one notorious one —

W. K. Vanderbilt's
mansion at Fifty-second
Street, ca. 1893.

46

had moved as far north as the Fifties in the early years of the boom. Mrs. Mary Mason Jones — Edith Wharton's cousin — built her French-style, pale marble mansion at Fifty-seventh Street in the 1860s, on land her father had bought several decades earlier. Her house stood in solitary splendor for some time, near unfinished streets only recently lit by gaslight. The infamous "Madam Restell," Mrs. Ann Lohman, New York's most famous abortionist, built a brownstone mansion on the northwest corner of Fifth Avenue and Fifty-second Street sometime in the 1850s. Although attempts were made to rid the neighborhood of Madam — it was said the cathedral was particularly embarrassed by her presence — she conducted her prosperous business from that unlikely location well into the 1870s, before she was arrested through a bit of trickery by police officer Anthony Comstock. Released on bail, she cut her throat several days later. Another New Yorker who relatively early on saw the promise of uptown was Hiram Cranston, owner of the New York Hotel. In 1865, he bought the block across from the entrance to Central Park, between Fifth and Madison avenues and Fifty-ninth and Sixtieth streets, intending to build a stylish hotel at what was sure to become, he felt, a new city crossroads.

By the time the city was well recovered from the depressions of the Civil War years, building was running wild and the Avenue was increasingly the place everyone with money or the hopes of it wanted to be. Building lots near the site of the growing cathedral sold for five times their prewar price, and narrow brownstone row houses, which gave the street, some thought, a "somber" look, went quickly for $125,000 and more. A gentleman bought a corner house on the Avenue in 1860 for $50,000 and furnished it for another $25,000. Nine years later he turned down an offer of $300,000 for his house, "believing," said a reporter, "that he would be able in a few years to command a still larger sum."[21]

Some observers took a haughty view of the crass businessmen and *nouveaux riches* who fought for a Fifth Avenue address — "a set of mere money getters and traders,"[22] Charles Francis Adams called them. Anthony Trollope observed:

"I know of no great man, no celebrated statesman, no philanthropist of note who has lived in Fifth Avenue. That gentleman on the right made a million dollars by inventing a shirt-collar; this one on the left electrified the world by a lotion; as to the gentleman at the corner there — there are rumours about him and the Cuban slave trade.... Such are the aristocracy of Fifth Avenue.[23]

The money to buy or build and to run a house — upkeep could be upwards of $25,00 a year in the mid-1860s — did come in various and occasionally suspect ways. "Many are here," James McCabe wrote,

who have strained every nerve to "get into the Avenue," and who would sell body and soul to stay there.... Others there are who would give half their possessions to move in the society in which their neighbors live. They reside on the Avenue, but they are ignored by one class of its occupants, because of their lack of refinement and cultivation, and by another because of their inferiority in wealth. Great wealth covers a multitude of defects in the Avenue.[24]

In the closing decades of the century, building along Fifth Avenue became a game for millionaires, and the stretch of spectacular private mansions that rose amid the churches was sometimes called Millionaire's Row or Two Miles of Millionaires. Goelets, Goulds, Huntingtons, Livingstons, Whitneys, Astors, and Waldorfs outdid each other in a series of Renaissance castles, French chateaux, and Italianate palazzos, complete with conservatories, libraries, grand staircases, reception halls to hold hundreds, art galleries, and, occasionally, bronze doors. About two years after the opening of St. Patrick's in 1879, William Henry Vanderbilt, son of Cornelius and supposedly the richest man in the world, started construction on three houses directly across the street from the cathedral, between Fifty-first and Fifty-second streets on the west side of Fifth Avenue. Huge brownstones in a Renaissance style, they required the labor of fifty foreign craftsmen and hundreds of local workers, and when they were finished William Henry took occupancy of one and moved two of his daughters—Mrs. William D. Sloane and Mrs. Elliot F. Shepard—into the others. He kept his horses at stables behind the cathedral at Fifty-second Street and Madison, held viewings of his $15-million collection of paintings, and set off a building spurt that turned that stretch of Fifth into a veritable warren of Vanderbilts for some years to come. His daughter-in-law, Mrs. William Kissam Vanderbilt—the unforgettable Alva—ordered a $3-million French-style palace in pale limestone to be erected north of Fifty-second Street, and from 660 Fifth, the costliest house on the Avenue, she organized entertainments that, finally, brought the Vanderbilts out of the class of "mere money getters" and established them as a social force to be reckoned with. Two other daughters of William Henry, Mrs. William Seward Webb and Mrs. Hamilton McKown Twombly, and another son, Cornelius II, carried the family enclave as far north as the recently laid out Grand Army Plaza, at the southern entrance to Central Park at Fifty-ninth Street.

Henry Villard, whose fortune came from the Northern Pacific Railroad, had built his brown sandstone house directly behind St. Patrick's on Madison Avenue. An Italian-style palazzo designed by McKim, Mead, and White and made up of a series of connecting mansions surrounding a large courtyard, it took up an entire block and turned out to be a little too much of a good thing for Mr. Villard. He was forced to sell part of it—for $500,000—to Darius Ogden Mills, who gave the mansion to his daughter, Mrs. Whitelaw Reid, as a wedding present.

By the time St. Patrick's was a working church, the streets around the cathedral marked the southern boundary of residential Fifth Avenue; those who could afford to live there were building farther and farther uptown, as far north as the Nineties along the east side of Central Park. Legitimate aristocracy—Hamilton Fish, who was President Grant's secretary of state, Mrs. Henry Phipps, Augustus Van Horne Stuyvesant, and Mrs. Astor — were mixing with the millionaire businessmen, such as Andrew Carnegie and Henry Clay Frick, and "downtown" once and for all had a new definition. The years during which St. Patrick's was built saw the area change from undesirable wilderness to the finest private address and, increasingly, to a center of commerce and trade.

Chapter 4:
Plans and Funds

James Renwick and Gothic Revival Architecture

In 1853, when Archbishop Hughes asked James Renwick to submit a plan for the new St. Patrick's Cathedral, the young architect—he was just 35 —was already the well-known designer of several important buildings. Ten years earlier he had won the competition to design Grace Church on Broadway and Fifth Street in New York, considered shortly after its opening in 1846 and ever since to be one of the masterpieces of Gothic Revival architecture. He followed his Grace Church work with the Romanesque-styled Smithsonian Institution in Washington, one of the great fantasy pieces of the time, and with a splendid private residence for C. T. Longstreet of Syracuse, a Gothic castle of immense proportions.

Oddly enough, Renwick had little training in architecture, and his early success and continued employment can be attributed in some measure not to his genius alone but to his prominent social position. His father, James, Sr., was professor of Natural and Experimental Philosophy and Chemistry at Columbia College, a Trustee of the college, and a serious watercolorist. His mother was a Brevoort, his wife was an Aspinwall, and his later life included the genteel pleasures of extensive travel in Europe, England, and Egypt and the maintenance of private steam yachts for fishing and cruising. His obituary listed him as "one of the oldest members of the Century and Union Clubs, and a prominent member of the New York and Larchmont Yacht Clubs."[1] Young Renwick's entry in the Grace Church competition was arranged by family friends, and it is startling to realize that this was his first major assignment. He had graduated from Columbia at eighteen, been appointed to an engineering position on the Erie Railroad, and then served as superintendent of the building of the Croton Aqueduct Distributing Reservoir at Forty-second Street and Fifth Avenue before his triumph at Grace Church, heart, soul, and pocketbook of mid-nineteenth-century New York Episcopal society.

Grace Episcopal was not the only Gothic-style structure in New York at the

Overleaf: Elevation of eastern end showing exterior of the Lady chapel as Renwick conceived it.

52

James Remwick
Architect

time. Indeed, the vogue for this elaborate form, derived from the age of great European cathedral building during the twelfth through the fifteenth centuries and encouraged in the 1830s and 40s by the romanticism of Henry Thoreau, Washington Irving, James Fenimore Cooper, and the Hudson River school of painters, had been growing since the early part of the century. Old St. Patrick's Cathedral on Mott and Prince streets, designed by Joseph Mangin and opened in 1815, was ornamented with Gothic details, and a number of country and townhouses, academic buildings and rectories displayed towers, balconies, wings, and oddly connecting rooms designed to appeal to the romantic imagination. The style seemed ideally suited to churches, as one commentator in the mid-1830s noted:

> *There is a style of architecture which belongs peculiarly to Christianity, and owes its existence even to this religion, whose very ornaments remind one of the joys of a life beyond the grave; whose lofty vaults and arches are crowded with the forms of prophets and martyrs and beatified spirits, and seem to resound with the choral hymns of angels and archangels. . .these are the characteristics of the architecture of Christianity, the sublime, the glorious Gothic.* [2]

Richard Upjohn's Trinity Church at Wall Street and Broadway, completed in 1846, showed the style in full flower and was an immediate popular and critical hit with admirers who praised its "almost medieval grandeur."[3] Built of reddish brownstone, with a single central tower, it set the style for churches across the country for a number of years. Trinity, Renwick's white marble Grace Church, and, of course, St. Patrick's are considered today highlights of America's Gothic Revival and have made familiar even to persons who have not seen the medieval cathedrals of Europe the dominant elements of that design—towering sandcastle spires; high, vaulted interiors; dramatically arched windows; delicate tracery work; ornaments of gargoyles, beasts, and saints.

Early Plans

The Roman Catholic archbishop, ministering largely to a congregation of poor immigrants, had found the right man to execute his "great undertaking," and in the summer of 1858 the accepted plans for the new St. Patrick's Cathedral were made public. Renwick's design was submitted in partnership with William Rodrigue, whose name is sometimes spelled in written accounts as Rodriguez, Rodrigues, and Rodrique. The extent of his participation is not clear. Rodrigue, who was distantly related to the archbishop by marriage, was involved in early meetings concerning the cathedral, and he, along with Renwick, was named in the contract with the church that stipulated the architects were to receive $2,500 a year for eight years. But Renwick drew the plans and it appears that Rodrigue had little further connection with the work, perhaps after a falling out between the two men.

According to the proposal, as reported in the *New York Times*, the building was to be constructed "in the most substantial manner" on the block between Fiftieth and Fifty-first streets, fronting on Fifth Avenue and reaching back "to where the line of Madison Avenue will run when that street is laid out at its upper end," a location that was considered "one of the most commanding and admirable on the whole island." Renwick estimated that, once work was "pushed on vigorously"[4] the following summer, enough of the building would be completed in three years to permit services to be held there. Renwick's original plan stated:

The building is to be a Gothic structure, on the plan of a Latin cross, 328 feet long and 175 feet wide. On each corner of the western front there are to be towers; the north tower to be capped with a painted tower, the other to bear a lofty openwork spire 333 feet in height from the pavement to the cross. A noble porch, deeply recessed and fringed with long pendants, will occupy the space between the towers; above all this will rise the gable to a height of 150 feet above the ground ornamented with a large rose window.

At a distance of 23 feet from the center immense buttresses will rise on the sides and the rear; these are to be constructed of solid masonry and will sustain the arches and vaulted roof; they are to terminate with foliated pinnacles and support the walls of the clerestory with graceful flying buttresses. Between each buttress in the side aisles and clerestory will be richly traceried windows. The church is to be entered by several flights of marble steps.[5]

Once inside, he continued,
a forest of marble columns will meet the eye. Fifty-seven clustered shafts will support the groined roof and bear the arches which divide the aisles. Nothing will intercept the view, and from the door to the apse which terminates the church, the high altar, approached by three flights of steps, will be the only conspicuous object to break the perspective. On either side of the altar there are to be chapels large enough to seat any ordinary congregation, and between each of the buttresses of the nave, which project outward sixteen feet, will be small chapels, giving a larger more airy appearance to the church.

The vault of the roof will be masonry—the only one of any size in the United States. No pews are to encumber the floor; the seats will be either free or, more probably, will be let out for each service, after the manner of the French or Italian churches.

Behind the high altar is to be a chapel of Our Lady. There will be no cellar or crypt. The building rests on solid rock and the floor will be simply leveled off and covered with marble.[6]

That completion of the building took closer to twenty years than to Renwick's estimated three is the most obvious discrepancy between the concept and the reality. But one of Renwick's first tasks was to reach agreement on the type of material to be used. He was "engaged in testing the merits of different kinds of stone,"[7] and in October presented to the archbishop an animated defense of the superiority of white marble over glazed or brown freestone, olive freestone, and granite. The white marble he had in mind was a material like granite, to be supplied by the East Chester Quarry of Mr. James Hall and Mr. William Joyce. He acknowledged that some might object to its color (and, indeed, in the then-current vogue for "natural" brownstone, it was not the critics' choice; in 1855, one magazine had called Renwick's Grace Church "a very showy building, very florid, and of bad white marble"[8]), but he defended his choice by citing the splendid marble cathedrals of Milan, Pisa, and Florence, which "satisfy the taste of the learned as well as the unlearned in ar-

Renwick's reputation as church architect extraordinaire is based on a long list of houses of worship, most of which are no longer standing:

Calvary Episcopal at Twenty-first Street and Fourth Avenue
Church of the Puritans in Union Square
Church of the Covenant at Forty-second Street
St. Mary's Episcopal Church in Washington (a recently designated landmark originally named St. Mary's Chapel for Colored People)
St. Bartholomew's on Madison Avenue and Forty-fourth Street
All Saints on Madison Avenue and One Hundred Twenty-ninth Street
St. Ann's Episcopal Church on Clinton Street in Brooklyn

But he designed, as well, a wide variety of secular buildings:

The Corcoran Gallery of Art in Washington, D.C.
The Workhouse, the City Hospital, and the Smallpox Hospital on Blackwell's Island, New York
The Inebriate Asylum and the Lunatic Asylum on Ward's Island, New York
The Children's Hospital on Randall's Island, New York
The Vassar Female College in Poughkeepsie, New York
The Clarendon, Albermarle, and St. Denis hotels, New York City

And luxurious private homes, country cottages, and "villas" in Staten Island, Dobbs Ferry, Tarrytown, New London, and Newport.

chitecture."[9] Contractors' statements placed the cost of this material at $50,000 higher than the lowest estimate for other stone, but Renwick felt its beauty and durability would more than justify the additional expense. The material, he wrote, was "almost a precious stone; every year will add to its beauty, and every turn of the setting sun will be reflected by the spires and pinnacles, and, thus forming a link with the colors of heaven, will produce the effect of carrying the mind of the beholder to the true object of the building—the worship of the Maker of the universe."[10] His argument was persuasive.

The job was given to Hall and Joyce, who agreed to build the cathedral for a cost of $850,000, including a marble exterior, brick vault, and everything else except the foundations, altars, and furnishings. The contract specified that the church would be finished on or before 1 January 1867, and that the builders "will not suffer or permit any spirituous liquors to be brought or used on said premises; that they shall instantly discharge any workman who may bring or use the same thereon, and that they will not knowingly employ any workman who shall live or board at any place in which spirituous liquors may be sold, within two blocks east or west, or four blocks north or south of said premises, under pain of forfeiture of this contract,"[11]

Laying the Cornerstone—the Work Begins

Grace Church.

Archbishop Hughes organized a solemn and splendid ceremony for laying the cornerstone on 15 August, the Feast of the Assumption, 1858. All the bishops of the province, in cape and miter, attended by their chaplains, one hundred boys in red cassocks, and surplices, priests, acolytes, St. Vincent de Paul members, and others were to be part of the grand procession. The archbishop wrote to Father Bernard Smith in Rome that the ceremony "on the scale which I have projected it will produce a sensation in this new country."[12] And it did. The *New York Times* called it a memorable day for New York.

From one o'clock until four the upcars were crammed almost beyond endurance. Nothing but the occasion could render the suffering tolerable. Not only were the cars crammed within, but without, the roofs were appropriated to a most threatening extent.

The Second, Third, Fourth, Sixth and Eighth Avenue railroads found themselves utterly inadequate to accommodate more than two-thirds of the applicants for seats. The Bowery, Broadway and the Sixth Avenues presented one almost unbroken line of carriages and the sidewalks were filled . . . .[13]

It was estimated that 100,000 people were on hand to witness Archbishop Hughes bless the stone and the place it was to be laid and, with a knife, mark the sign of the cross on each side of the stone. In his address, the archbishop recalled the history of persecution that attended the spiritual descendants of St. Patrick, "outcasts from their native land," and talked movingly of the earliest beginnings of the Church in New York:

Next to Almighty God the cornerstone of this Cathedral is to be laid under the auspices of the Immaculate Virgin Mary. Its special patron is announced as the glorious Apostle of Ireland, St. Patrick, originally selected as patron of the first Cathedral commenced by our Catholic ancestors in Mott Street, fifty-two years ago. Their undertaking was indeed an example of zeal and enterprise worthy of our commendation. They were few, they were very poor; but their efforts were as large as the Cathedral which they projected, and theirs were the hearts of great men. It might be said of them . . . that "There were giants in those days."[14]

After the ceremonies a number of the dignitaries enjoyed an evening's entertainment in the refectory of the nearby orphan asylum, and "there was no exception," the *Times* reported, "to the general satisfaction." Archbishop Hughes expressed his pleasure that there had been no disorder or accidents in the large crowd, and that the secular papers spoke of the ceremony "with kindest feelings of praise and admiration."[15]

Paying for St. Patrick's

I n a cavity of the cornerstone was placed a document on which were listed the names of the first patrons of the cathedral, a group of 101 leading Catholic gentlemen of the city and two non-Catholics, each of whom had pledged to support the building operations with $1,000. The pledges were the strikingly successful result of the archbishop's petition, the first part of his overall plan for financing what was by then estimated to be five years of construction work, and only the beginning of a series of imaginative fund-raising efforts carried out during and after the archbishop's lifetime and leading to the consecration of the debt-free cathedral in 1910. In June 1858, while discussions with the architects and contractors were still going on, Archbishop Hughes appealed by letter to the prominent New York citizens who were, he wrote, "those only who may be able and disposed under noble impulses" to aid him in his plans for "the great new St. Patrick's Cathedral."[16] His letter was written, he continued, "to ascertain whether there are not in my Diocese, or rather in the city of New York itself, one hundred persons who will subscribe $1,000 each, once and for all, to be paid in quarterly installments, if they desire it, during the first year, and to be expressly and exclusively appropriated to carry on the work during the same period."[17]

No further appeal for funds, he said, would be made for a year after the cornerstone laying on 15 August. After that time, he intended to ask for an additional $100,000, calling on persons who could not afford to contribute $1,000 but would be asked for not less than $100 each. The success of the second year he expected would depend on that of the first, and if all went as planned, he anticipated "there should not be a single suspension of the work. . . . My principle is to pay as we proceed, up to an amount of half a million dollars; and if at that point it should be necessary to obtain a loan of two or three hundred thousand dollars, I do not think that this need frighten anyone. But I should not wish it to be consecrated in my lifetime until it is finished from the foundation stone to the top of the cross on the uplifted spires."[18]

He thanked these 103 first patrons in his sermon at the cornerstone-laying ceremony for their support, for the zeal and generosity that successive contributors would look to as an example to emulate, and for saving him "from the necessity of begging." And he warned that "those who are of this world"

At the time of the Cathedral's construction, the giant stones were hauled in wagons pulled by horses and mules, since there was no mechanized transportation at that time. A sudden equine epidemic swept the city, and all hauling stopped while the disease raged. The final stones of St. Patrick's were slowly carted through the city streets by lumbering teams of oxen, who were brought in from neighboring farms.

might accuse them of extravagance, saying the money should go to the poor, but how much better to give the mechanic and laborer "honorable employment" than alms for the relief of poverty.[19]

The cathedral actually collected somewhat over $70,000 of those pledges, enough to lay the foundations and raise the exterior walls to a height of about sixteen feet. But in August 1860, just two years after his triumphant beginning, Archbishop Hughes announced that construction would be temporarily suspended. He had run out of money, and, he wrote in a letter to the *Times*, "it is known to all the Catholics of New York that, whether it should ever be completed or not, I will never allow the laborer to be defrauded of his wages in carrying on the work, and, consequently, whenever the funds are too low to pay the laborer the work must stop." He had not put into action the second part of his money-raising plan, but many people were out of town, the weather was hot, his own health was not robust, and, on the whole, he thought it was not "much to be regretted that the building should have a little repose, and time to settle on its foundations."[20]

The Civil War effectively lengthened that "little repose." John Hughes was shortly involved in secular missions in the United States and abroad pertaining to the war, and he died, in January 1864, without seeing further construction progress. But his successor, Archbishop John McCloskey, later the first American cardinal, proved to be equally enthusiastic about the promise of the cathedral and to possess the perseverance and financial acumen to see the job to completion. He ordered the building resumed shortly after the war, and was apparently a spiritual leader of such effectiveness that the necessary funds were found. A newspaper editorial in 1875, chastising the city's Protestant population for its unwillingness to make personal sacrifices on behalf of its religion, applauded what it perceived as Catholic generosity: "Even now, the noblest ecclesiastical building ever erected in this City, or in the United States, is slowly going up in Fifth Avenue, and where does the money for it come from? Largely out of the pockets of poor Irish servants, some of whom we have known to give as much as five or eight dollars a month out of their wages to this one special object."[21]

The building was nearly completed—there were as yet no spires and no interior furnishings—when, in 1878, Cardinal McCloskey initiated the most sweeping fund-raising effort of all: the St. Patrick's Fair. It opened on 23 October, ran for a month, was documented in a daily twelve-page tabloid called *Journal of the Fair*, and was called by the *New York Times* "the grandest display of the kind that has been seen in the City since the great fairs of war times, when all New York gathered in the academy of music and passed out money like water for the soldiers."[22] Months of preparation had occupied 1,400 volunteer ladies; forty-six parishes from various parts of the diocese sponsored tables, at which were sold or raffled hand-embroidered cloths, jewelry, religious paintings, "rare conceits in gold, silver, bronze and porcelain," a gilt and ebony screen, furs, "many dainty articles of virtu," a $500 parlor set from the Brooklyn Furniture Company, and an exquisite christening robe from Bloomingdale Brothers.[23]

During the day the fair was attended mainly by ladies—who, one of the table attendants complained, never wanted to take more than a twenty-five-cent chance—and by hordes of school children. At night, the festivities were lit by 1,400 gas jets and enlivened by a musical group named Garfulla's Band, which "rendered choice selections of the sweetest music."[24] There was a floral pavilion, a refreshment room, a machinery hall, a demonstration of Edison's phonograph, and a shooting gallery, as well as a post office at which one could buy a correspondence "from the realms of fancy or romance or the mysterious domain of poetry."[25] Among the prizes were a sod of turf cut near Dublin, a 25-by-100 foot piece of property on Long Island, a ton of coal, and a Cuban pony. There were contests, decided by purchased votes, for the most popular pastor, the most popular police inspector (who won a gold-and-diamond badge), and the most popular Civil War general—the prize of a gold-and-silver, diamond-studded sword was won by General Wylie. Over 20,000 people came to opening night, and, at month's end, the fair had collected $172,625 to further the building of St. Patrick's.

Although James Renwick had envisioned a church without pews, with free-standing seats in the European manner, by the time the cathedral was opened in May 1879, pews of polished ash had been put in place and were ready for occupancy and for rental at public auction. A reporter referred to "the necessity of the Church to be self-supporting and the fact that it could be made so only by renting pews"[26] as the probable cause for the change in seating plans. In any case, on the evening of 30 May, 53 of the "choicest" pews were sold *in perpetuo* at prices ranging from $50 to $2,100. Each purchaser was to retain ownership of the pew during his lifetime, after which it could be passed on to his family, but pews could not be sold or parted with in any way and were to be maintained at annual rents ranging from $100 to $150 each. Of the 365 pews in the cathedral, 98 alone were not to be rented.

The matter of the cathedral debt continued to occupy the attention of church officials, and in 1894 a bazaar was opened in the Grand Central Palace, or the Palace of Industry, on Lexington Avenue, by then Archbishop Corrigan. A less extensive festivity than the original, it was nonetheless a lively affair with a maze, another post office, and all sorts of items to be raffled, from bicycles to diamond rings. The profits were to be devoted exclusively to paying the floating debt on St. Patrick's.

It was, finally, Archbishop John Farley who saw John Hughes' vision into the twentieth century and engineered and inspired, in 1909 and 1910, the final drive "to release our Cathedral from the last claim of man"[27] and free it for consecration. In an action reminiscent of that of his earliest predecessor, Archbishop Farley called—by taxicab—on a number of prominent Roman Catholics of the city asking what help they could give in settling the approximately half-million dollar debt remaining. Several businessmen contributed $25,000 each; a number of others pledged large single amounts, and, in all, individual supporters gave more than $220,000. Another $300,000 was the gift of the clergy and laity of the archdiocese of New York to Archbishop Farley on the fortieth anniversary of his ordination to the priesthood. He was able to plan "the happy consummation of more than half a century of toil and anxious care."[28]

Construction work, 1869.

The Work Continues and the Cathedral Opens

When Archbishop McCloskey ordered construction on the cathedral resumed at the end of the Civil War, the building resembled a large open box. The foundations, huge blocks of gneiss, and the base course of Maine granite had been completed some years earlier; the walls —almost four feet thick—had risen to a height of about two stories. By 1869, work was once again in full swing. Marble was brought to the site by a specially constructed branch of the Harlem Railroad from the Pleasantville quarries, and the large blocks, weighing ten to fifteen tons each, lay about the surrounding field.

A reporter from the *Bergen County Democrat* gave his impressions of the construction about two years later.[29] The elaborately carved and ornamented facade and main entrance facing Fifth Avenue were complete. The great doorway "looked as though it were carved in snow." Inside the empty building, the ground was covered with grass and weeds. Piles of debris, great marble blocks, piles of bricks and cement were scattered about. Work was proceeding "in a dreamy sort of way." A single horse was carrying bricks and mortar to the men outside. A plodding yoke of oxen was slowly moving blocks of marble on a low sledge. "One has an almost irresistible inclination to lie down and go to sleep somewhere about the place."

The work got done, though, and by 1879 the great oak doors were in place, the windows and organ were installed, and the high altar was completed. Only the spires were needed to finish the main exterior of the building. (Renwick's plan for a Lady chapel extending out behind the main altar had been temporarily abandoned.) When the cathedral was opened for worship, the spires stopped on a level with the roof, but in 1885 architect Renwick filed plans for the erection of two Gothic spires, "to correspond with the style of the building which they are to adorn,"[30] and by 1888 they were completed, at a cost of about $200,000. On an evening in that year, Archbishop Corrigan was called from his study to watch the cross on the north spire being fixed in place, at last. No ceremony marked the occasion; it was the quiet end of a noble beginning.

A very different scene had prevailed nine years earlier, when his predecessor Cardinal McCloskey presided at the formal opening and dedication of St. Patrick's Cathedral, on 25 May 1879, the feast if St. Gregory VII. It was "a propitious day," the *Tribune* reported,[31] with bright skies and cool breezes that added to the comfort of the thousands who watched the proceedings, part of which took place outside. Workmen had been caught in a final frenzy of activity for several months, finishing painting and carpentry work, laying a sidewalk along the Fifth Avenue entrance, clearing the grounds of rubbish, and cleaning up. A reporter visiting the cathedral a week before its opening was impressed by how "marvelously fresh and neat" the interior looked, especially since large portions of it had been standing roofless and exposed for the previous thirteen or fourteen years. "The accumulations of dust, the weather stains, the dirt and splashes which come with the progress of the work, have

Three archbishop's who built St. Patrick's (top to bottom): John Cardinal McCloskey, Archbishop Michael Augustine Corrigan, and John Cardinal Farley.

St. Patrick's Cathedral in 1878, as it neared completion. (Below) A *carte-de-visite* photograph, taken about 1860, showing St. Patrick's under construction.

Back view of the cathedral, before the Lady chapel was added.

all been carefully removed. The stained-glass windows have been cleaned, the walls dusted, the stone-work rubbed with steel brushes until the whole interior of the great building looks as pure and spotless as if it were the magic creation of a night and had risen with the morning."[32]

The opening ceremony started at ten and lasted until about three. The *Times* reported:

The bright sunshine streamed through the stained glass windows, lighting up the chaste and elegantly modeled interior with clearness hardly inferior to that outside the broad marble walls. The space between the pews and the sanctuary swarmed with representatives of the press from all over the country and Canada.

Far off in the extreme distance, as viewed from the sanctuary rails, up rose the beautifully curved and painted pipes of the grand organ, the wide loft below being apparently packed to repletion with the "hundred mixed voices" which were to assist the double quartet in interpreting the figured music of the Mass. . . .

High up among the capitals of the great supporting columns, a number of sparrows flitted and twittered. The little fellows, though not in the programme, managed to make themselves a conspicuous feature of the entire proceedings.[33]

A continuous double line of policemen surrounded the building, admitting first holders of purple tickets, who were seated inside by ushers; later in the proceedings, holders of blue standing-room-only tickets were allowed in.

When the full complement of ticket holders was inside, the *Times* estimated there were not less than 7,000 persons in the great building. The great procession of thirty-five bishops, six archbishops, priests and other religious, led by Cardinal McCloskey, started from the Church of St. John the Evangelist behind the cathedral on Madison Avenue, entered the doors behind the main altar, and walked through the church to the front entrance, where the cardinal blessed the central doorway. The grand procession circled the block as the cardinal sprinkled the cathedral walls with holy water and the choir sang the Miserere. The ritual was repeated inside the building, after which Cardinal McCloskey was rerobed in the appropriate garments for the celebration of High Mass. His vestment included "a pair of red jeweled sandals. The new outer robes were like the others, off-white silk heavily embroidered with gold and graceful designs, but they were incomparably richer and were studded all over with precious stones."[34] The Right Reverend Patrick John Ryan, co-adjutor bishop of St. Louis, who was called the greatest preacher in the Roman Catholic Church, gave the sermon, which lasted for over two hours, and at the end of the Mass the Vicar General announced that regular services in St. Patrick's would begin the following Sunday. Almost thirty years after John Hughes first had his dream, years during which the country survived a civil war and midtown New York had evolved from a remote countryside, the great cathedral was finally open for worship.

Chapter 5:
The Building

St. Patrick's Cathedral was built in the decorated and geometric style of Gothic architecture, of which the European and English cathedrals at Rheims, Amiens, Cologne, York Minster, Exeter, and Westminster are the outstanding examples. To each of those, and others as well, James Renwick's building has been compared. French parentage is seen in the twin spires, the plan of nave and aisles, details about the windows and doors. The interior elevation, the ceiling vaulting, aspects of the side chapels are said to be purely English in inspiration. Renwick himself drew comparisons to the great cathedrals of Italy and Germany.

Not all St. Patrick's watchers have been pleased with the results. Shortly before the cathedral opened, the *Daily Tribune* reported[1] that "it goes sorely against the grain with us to be unable to praise cordially and unreservedly the structure as thus far finished." The paper did not hold the architect entirely to blame, certain that he had been hampered by lack of money, by changes to his original design, and by the selection of a piece of ground far too small for the purpose. We can only look to Europe for comparison, the reporter went on, but "alas! the time we fear is forever gone by when we can hope to do more than to touch the outermost hem of the garment of the glory of the past." The new cathedral, according to Archbishop Hughes, was meant to have been, at least, superior in size, but "though it is a large church for America, where there are no large churches, it is not a large church for Europe." If ever its spires were completed, the *Tribune* thought, they, anyway, would be "respectable" by European standards. This disgruntled observer found the exterior "unfortunately ill-digested, and made ineffective by the multiplication of petty parts"; the moldings "clumsy in design and coarse in execution"; the building material "a very mistaken one" for the delicate style of the ornamentation; and the principal doorway—well, unspeakable: "Let those who wish to judge it compare it with the door, we will not say of any one of the great cathedrals, for that would be superfluous malice but with the door of almost any parish church in England built in the good time of architecture."

The *New York Times* was somewhat less testy but also not entirely satisfied,

Overleaf: Detail from window of the Blessed Virgin, north transept. (Right) Mourners crowd around the cathedral for the funeral of Cardinal McCloskey, 24 October 1885. Note the absence of the spires, which were not to be added to the edifice for another three years. (From the cover of *Harper's Weekly*)

thinking Mr. Renwick had "given a fair but not a thorough example"[2] of the decorated Gothic style. Two of the complaints raised were legitimate and ones with which Renwick would himself have agreed. His provisions for an aisle running around the apse and leading to a chapel behind the main altar had been revised by Archbishop Hughes, perhaps because he felt the ground covered by them would be needed for the residences of the archbishop and clergy. The east end of the church thus ended abruptly in a flat wall behind the altar, a graceless form with which no one was particularly happy. Renwick also protested the use of plaster rather than stone in the vaulted ceiling, making unnecessary the flying buttresses he had designed to abut the vaults.

Some thought the cathedral "rather stiff," not one of Renwick's best works, heavy in feeling. But they were few. At the time and in the years since, the great majority—professional critics and laymen, religious, tourists—have looked at St. Patrick's and found it dignified, spacious, chaste, beautiful, imposing.

The General Plan

The plan of the church building follows the lines of the Latin cross: the vestibule, or narthex, with the main entrances at Fifth Avenue and the nave, or body of the church, make up the long arm of the cross; the areas running north and south about midway down the length of the building and opening onto Fifty-first Street and Fiftieth Street are called the transepts, and constitute the short arms of the cross. Where the nave and transepts cross each other begins the area of the church containing the clergy choir, the sanctuary, and the high altar. Directly behind the altar is the polygonal apse, beyond which can be seen the Lady chapel.

The body of the cathedral contains three aisles, the central one called the nave and the two side ones called, technically, the aisles. The nave leads to the communion rail; the aisles extend beyond the transepts and continue around the high altar in a semicircular path called the ambulatory. The entrance to the Lady chapel begins at the center of the ambulatory. Directly behind the high altar are the steps that lead to the crypt and the sacristies. Running along the exterior walls, bordering each aisle and adjacent to the marble columns of the nave, are ten recessed alcoves against the exterior walls which contain eight small chapels, or side altars, and, nearest the vestibule, the baptistry on the north side and the cathedral library, or pamphlet room, on the south. The

(Top right) Detail from architect Renwick's drawing of the longitudinal section of St. Patrick's Cathedral. (Right) The great bronze doors at the main entrance of the cathedral. The doors were designed by Charles D. Maginnis; the figures are the work of John Angel, a British sculptor. At the top are depicted our Lord, the twelve apostles, the Blessed Virgin Mary, and St. John the Baptist. The figures in the doors are: (top row) St. Joseph and St. Patrick; (middle row) St. Isaac Jogues and St. Frances X. Cabrini; (lower row) Venerable Kateri Tekakwitha and Mother Elizabeth Seton.

SAINT JOSEPH   PATRON OF THE CHURCH   SAINT PATRICK   PATRON OF THIS CHURCH

ST ISAAC JOGUES MARTYR   FIRST PRIEST IN NEW YORK   ST FRANCES X CABRINI   MOTHER OF THE IMMIGRANT

VEN KATERI TEKAKWITHA   LILY OF THE MOHAWKS   MOTHER ELIZ BETH SETON   DAUGHTER OF NEW YORK

north and south transepts each contain an altar, and three additional altars share the sanctuary aisles with the chancel organ. Finally, the Lady chapel is flanked by two semioctagonal chapels and altars leading off the ambulatory, which gives access also on the north to a small usher's office and on the south to the archbishop's sacristy. The congregation is seated in the nave, the aisles, and both the transepts. The seating capacity is approximately 3,000 but the cathedral can accommodate over 5,000 persons.

Facade

*A*s in all proper Gothic cathedrals, the principal entrance to St. Patrick's faces west. The Fifth Avenue front consists of a central gable with tower and spire to each side of it. The grand portal in the lower part of the central gable displays jambs decorated with columns having foliated capitals, clustered moldings, and an ornamented arch over the entrance fringed with a double row of foliated tracery. The arched area above the door opening, called the tympanum, forms a window filled with tracery.

In the center of the richly panelled small gable, or gablet, over the main entrance is a shield bearing the coat of arms of Archbishop Hughes—his cross, the miter, the clerical hat with tassels, and his motto. The gable itself displays a design of grapevine and morning glory about the outer molding. The main entrance and the two on each side of it are flanked with buttresses, four of which terminate in eight-foot colonnetted niches that will eventually contain statues. Between the double buttresses on each side of the central door are wall niches holding, on the left, a statue of the Blessed Virgin and, on the right, a statue of St. Joseph, the earthly father of Christ. Above the smaller entrance on the Fiftieth Street side is the shield of the State of New York; above the one near Fifty-first Street is a shield carrying the arms of the United States.

A horizontal row of traceried panels, like a balustrade, is to be seen above the Fifth Avenue entrances and running around the entire cathedral. This architectural treatment defines the location of the triforium, or first-floor level, inside the church. At this level over the main entrance is a row of six niches, to be filled eventually with statues, and above these niches begins the enframement of the splendid rose window, equal in size to the rose windows of some of the great cathedrals of Europe. Above the rose window the main gable, veiled by a pierced screen of rich tracery and decorated with a design of the passion flower, rises to the roof line.

The two square towers on either side of the main gable are divided below the roof line into three stories. The first contains the portal entrances; a shield over the Fiftieth Street portal shows a cross with a rose, and over the Fifty-first Street portal the shield has a cross with a crown of thorns. The second has tall windows, approximately on a level with the rose window; and the third has four small windows that open into the beginning of the bell loft. Where the tower ends, about 136 feet from the base, the octagonal chamber called the lantern of the tower begins. The eight faces of each lantern are filled with windows, and the eight corners end in pinnacles. Finally, above each lantern rises the octagonal, two-storied spire. Tracery panelling covers each pyramidal surface up about half the height of the spire, at which point a ring of small gables begins the second story, leading to the cross.

The side walls of the cathedral running the length of Fiftieth and Fifty-first streets show the main divisions of the nave, the transepts, and the sanctuary. The nave section of this facade is made up of five bays separated vertically by buttresses with open niches and pinnacles at the top. Horizontally, the facade has two main divisions, in the first of which are a series of twenty-four windows that light the side aisles inside above their chapels. The windows that light the nave, transepts, and sanctuary make up the second division, which is called the clerestory and which rises thirty-eight feet above the roof of the side aisles. The clerestory has six bays along the nave, two in each transept sidewall, three in the sanctuary, and five in the apse. There are forty windows, including the rose window, at this level.

The entrances of the two transepts correspond in general design to the portals of the Fifth Avenue facade. Their outer bronze doors and enframement show in the lower panels the coats of arms of the first four archbishops of the New York archdiocese. Over each door the great transept windows fill the whole space up to the end of the gable. Buttresses flank the transept entrances, including flying buttresses at the sides, and each transept facade terminates in an octagonal pinnacle and a foliated cross.

Beyond the transepts are the bays that define the sanctuary, and the next series of windows forms with their walls and buttresses the rear of the cathedral at the clerestory level, or the apse. All the windows on the upper division of this facade are surmounted by small, traceried gables, and these gables penetrate the ornamented battlement at the eaves, as do the pinnacles of the adjacent buttresses.

The Bronze Doors

The splendid bronze doors leading into the cathedral—two in the north tower, two in the south tower, and the central, or ceremonial, door — were dedicated in December 1949 by Cardinal Spellman in celebration of the 100th anniversary of the archdiocese of New York. Designed by architect Charles D. Maginnis with statuary sculpted by John Angel, they replaced the wooden doors of Renwick's church. The central doors are 16 feet 6¼ inches wide, weigh 10,000 pounds each, and are operated on a specially designed pivot. Just above them the figure of Christ the Redeemer looks out, surrounded by the twelve apostles, the Virgin Mary, St. John the Baptist and two angels with scrolls.

The doors themselves display six figures, each thirty-seven inches high and flanked by a decorative design, and each identified in some way with the church and the State of New York. St. Joseph, the upper left statue, holds a budding staff, token of his espousal to the Virgin Mary, and a carpenter's square, symbolic of the saint as patron of workingmen. The design to his left refers to his position as earthly father of Christ and patron of the universal Church; to his right the design is symbolic of his purity of life and intention.

St. Patrick, patron of the archdiocese of New York and apostle of Ireland,

(Top) Detail of the lantern of the tower, south spire. (Bottom) Exterior view of the great rose window, west entrance to the cathedral.

stands in the upper right section. On his left is the mystical phoenix rising to renewed life and the word *gratis* ("gratitude"). On his right is the Celtic harp and the word *laus* ("praise").

The middle left figure is that of St. Isaac Jogues, the French Jesuit priest who was the first Catholic missionary to enter New York State. He holds a crucifix, representative of his mission to the Iroquois. The palm branch to his left is a martyr's symbol. The Greek letters *ICXC* and the word *nika* mean "Jesus Christ conquers"; the word *passio* means "passion." The other panel has a chalice and the letters *AMDG*, which stand for the Latin motto of the Society of Jesus.

The middle right figure is that of Mother Cabrini, wearing the habit of the Missionary Sisters of the Sacred Heart, which she founded. To her left, the dolphin and star symbolize Pope Leo XIII's direction to extend her apostolic work to the West; the word *spes* means "hope." Two hands and a rose represent her heart going out to the immigrant; *cor* and *Jesu* mean "heart of Jesus."

In the lower left of the door stands the Venerable Kateri Tekakwitha, an Indian maiden known as the Lily of the Mohawks. The design to her left shows an American eagle with the word *fides* ("faith"). To her right is the coat of arms of Pope Pius XII, who declared her venerable in 1943, with his motto *Opus Justitae Pax*, "Peace is the work of justice."

The statuette in the lower right is of St. Elizabeth Ann Seton, canonized the first American-born saint in 1975. The panel to her right shows a rose-bush, for the official state flower, and the word *caritas*, ("charity"). On her left is the heraldic charge of Cardinal Spellman with his motto *Sequere Deum*, "Follow God."

The Bells

The bells of St. Patrick greet the morning at eight o'clock, sound the noonday angelus, and wish city workers safely home at five o'clock. The story behind their mellifluous chimes is one of the fascinating tales of the cathedral. Considered among the finest sets of chimes in the country, the nineteen bells—donated by individuals and Catholic groups—stand in the northern spire of the cathedral, 160 feet above ground level. As the system was originally conceived, the bellringer would climb a narrow spiral staircase entered by way of a small door off the church side entrance. One hundred ten upward feet of darkness later, he would stumble onto a platform halfway up the spire. On this platform a ringing arrangement that might have been designed by Rube Goldberg after a talk with Quasimodo produced the hymns and tolls of St. Patrick's.

A giant keyboard 8 feet long and equipped with nineteen wooden levers was "played" by the ringer. Attached to each lever was a leather strap connected to a wooden rod. Each rod, 110 feet long, ran up the spire to the clappers of one of the bells. As a lever was pressed—and this involved considerable physical effort—the strap would cause the rod to strike the clapper. The system worked and, until the electronic age overcame us, was considered adequate.

The Bells of St. Patrick's

NAME	TONE	DONOR
St. Patrick	B♭	cathedral
Blessed Virgin	C	parishioners Jon. B. Manning
St. Joseph	D	Jos. J. O'Donahue
Holy Name	E♭	Holy Name Sodality Societies
St. Michael	E	Michael S. Coleman
St. Anne	F	Henry McAleenan
St. Elizabeth	G	Marquise de San Marzano
St. Augustine	A♭	Augustus Daly
St. Anthony of Padua	A	Memory of Edward Fox
St. Agnes	B♭	Memory of Jas. Edward Fox
St. John the Evangelist	B	John D. Crimmins
St. Bridget	C	Memory of Aloysia Miniter
St. Francis Xavier	C#	The Catholic Club
St. Peter	D	George B. Coleman
St. Cecelia	E♭	Mrs. Thomas F. Ryan
St. Helena	E	Eleonora Keyes
St. Alphonsus Liguori	F	Maria A. Mills
St. Thomas Aquinas	F#	Thomas Kelly
St. Godfrey	G	Memory of John & Mary Koop

Today, the keyboard is a miniature piano with nineteen keys; no climbing is necessary unless one wishes to see the magnificent set of bells. The keyboard is in three hexagonal decks, according to tone—bass on the bottom, middle tone next, and upper register atop.

Commissioned in France, the bells are made of two parts of copper to one part tin, although cathedral tradition says there is also silver, at least in the voice of the bells.

The cost of the bells remains a matter of confidence between the cathedral and the donors. Each bell is inscribed with the name of the donor and a verse in Latin and English.

When they were installed in 1897, Archbishop Corrigan in an unusual church ceremony blessed them with a "Baptism of the Bells," whereby he washed each bell in holy water and anointed the inside of each with chrism, the outside with oil. The largest of the bells is named, appropriately, for St. Patrick, and is inscribed: "Your Patrick, I; As your sires, so also ye; Ever be, Emulators, imitators of me."

The Interior

Inside the cathedral the nave is defined by two rows of piers, six on each side, made up of clustered columns. These columns support by means of arches the great walls of the clerestory and the roof of the building. Above the arches runs an arcade, apparent as a screen with four openings, tracery, mullions, and decorated panels. This arcade is called the triforium and is reached by a stair in the south transept. The triforium traditionally provided an area in the Gothic cathedral in which the cloistered religious orders could attend service and still maintain their isolation. Above the triforium arcade rise the clerestory windows, made up of four arched divisions topped by circular Gothic-styled panels. The windows penetrate the arch of the great vaulted ceiling, lighting the far recesses of the roof.

From the central part of the nave piers, emerging from the columns, a colonnette runs up past the arches of the nave and past the triforium to end at the clerestory windows in a deeply carved capital. The graceful arch lines that form the vault and ceiling of the cathedral spread out from these capitals, the vault beginning near the top of the capitals some seventy-seven feet above the church floor. The ceiling is groined with ribs that have foliated bosses at their intersections.

These main elements of the nave—the arches formed by the columns, the triforium arcade, the clerestory windows, the vaulted ceiling—are carried through in the architectural treatment of the transept, sanctuary, ambulatory, and apse walls.

The side aisles running adjacent to the nave also are vaulted, these vaults formed by arches rising from the nave piers and clustered pilasters, which are part of the rectangular piers that both define the side chapels and support the triforium. The flat arches that form openings into the side chapels are directly below the windows of the side aisles, which are similar in design to the clerestory windows.

Marble tracery from the sanctuary.

Chapter 6:
A Walking Tour of the Cathedral

1 Window
St. Vincent de Paul

2 Chapel and Altar,
St. Anthony of Padua

3 Window
St. Andrew,
St. Elizabeth
and St. Catherine of
Alexandria

4 Chapel and Altar
St. John and Evangelist

5 Window
The Annunication

6 Shrine
St. Elizabeth Ann Seton

7 Window
St. Henry

8 Chapel and Altar
St. Rose of Lima

9 Window
Pope Pius IX

10 Window
James Renwick's gift

11 Window
Sacred Heart

12 Window
St. Louis,
King of France

13 Window
St. Luke

14 Window
Life of St. Patrick

15 Window
St. John

16 Altar of the
Blessed Sacrament

17 Window
Sacrifice of Abraham

18 Chapel and Altar
St. Andrew

19 Window
St. Anges, St. Thomas,
and St. James

20 Window
Eating of the Paschal
Lamb

21 Altar of
St. Theresa,
Little Flower

22 Window
St. Alphonsus Liguori,
St. Theresa, St. Susanna

23 Window
Death of St. Joseph

24 Archbishop's
Sacristy

25 Window
Sacrifice of Calvary

26 Pieta

27 Chapel and Altar
of St. Elizabeth

28 The Crypt

29 The High Altar
and Baldachin

30 The Apsidal
Windows

31 The Lady Chapel

32 Altar of
St. Michael and
St. Louis

33 Window
Sacrifice of
Melchisedech

34 Window
Nativity of Christ

35 Window
Adoration of the
Child Jesus

36 Chapel and Altar
St. Joseph

37 Window
Sacrifice of Noe

38 Chancel Organ

39 Window
Presentation
of the
Blessed Virgin

40 Window
Sacrifice of Abel

41 Altar
The Holy Family

42 Window
St. Monica and
St. Augustine

43 Window
St. Matthew

44 Window
Life of the Blessed Virgin

45 Window
St. Mark

46 Window
St. Paul

47 Window
St. Charles Borromeo

48 Window
St. Bernard

49 Chapel and Altar
Holy Relics

50 Shrine
St. John Neumann

51 Window
Martyrdom of
St. Lawrence

52 Window
Pope Benedict XIII

53 Chapel and Altar
St. Jean Baptiste
de la Salle

54 Chapel and Altar
St. Brigid and
St. Bernard

55 Window
St. Columbanus

56 Window
The Three Baptisms

57 The Baptistry

58 The Organ

59 The Rose Window

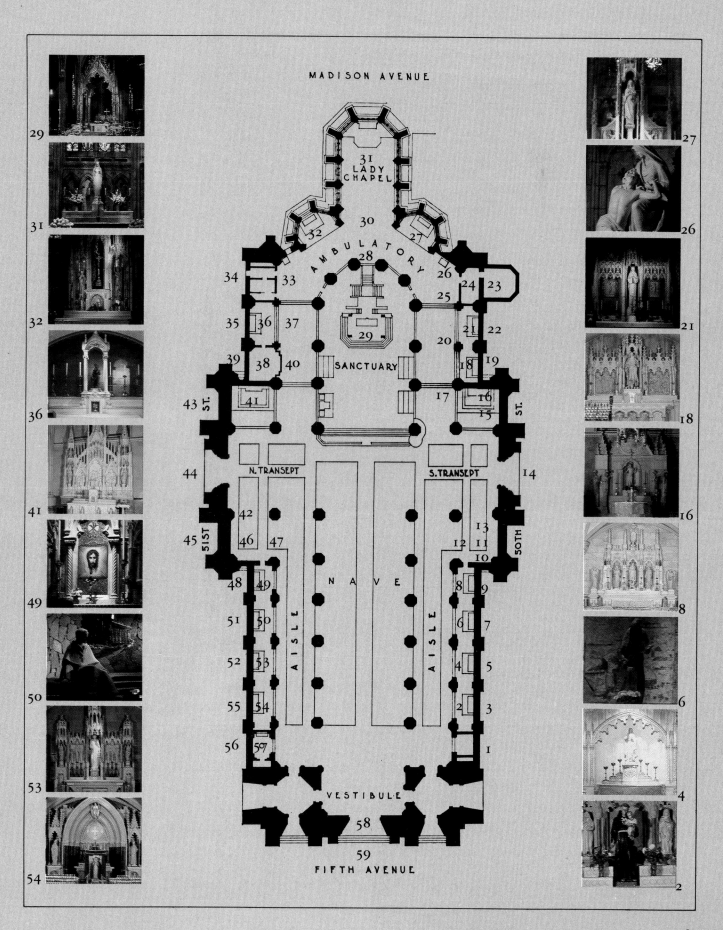

MADISON AVENUE

31
LADY
CHAPEL

30

32   27

AMBULATORY

28

34   33   26

24 23

25

35   36   37   20   21 22

SANCTUARY   18 19

39 38   40   29   17   16

43 ST.   41   15

ST.

N. TRANSEPT   S. TRANSEPT   14

44

42   13

45 51ST   46   47   12 11   50TH

48   49   NAVE   10

AISLE   AISLE   8 9

51   50   6 7

52   53   4 5

55   54   2 3

56   57   1

VESTIBULE

58

59

FIFTH AVENUE

29

31

32

36

41

49

50

53

54

27

26

21

18

16

8

6

4

2

The visitor entering St. Patrick's at the Fifth Avenue main door turns right past the vestibule and approaches the cathedral pamphlet rack, a room devoted to current Catholic literature. The library was added in 1931, from a design by Robert J. Reilly, architect.

The window over this chapel is devoted to St. Vincent de Paul, founder of the Vincentian Fathers and the Sisters of Charity. In the central division stands a full-sized figure of the saint as Messenger of Charity, wearing stole and surplice. The adjacent panels of the window show scenes of his heroic service to the poor and unfortunate—on the left, St. Vincent directs a Sister of Charity to a little waif on the pavement.

The South Aisle

Moving toward the sanctuary along the south aisle, the next alcove the visitor passes contains the chapel and altar of St. Anthony of Padua. In the center of the reredos—the ornamental screen, or panel, behind the altar—a relief carving shows St. Anthony with the infant Jesus.

The window above the chapel displays full-length figures of three saints. In the central division, St. Andrew the Apostle, brother of St. Peter, receives the cross of his martyrdom; the scene of his death is portrayed in the smaller panel. The figure in the left-hand section of the window is St. Elizabeth of Hungary, who carried in her cloak bread for the poor that turned into roses. In the window division to the right is the figure of St. Catherine of Alexandria. Beheaded at the age of eighteen, she holds the palm branch, symbol of victory, in her left hand and leans on the wheel upon which she was tortured. Beneath is the scene of her spiritual espousal to Christ, based on a painting by Peter Paul Rubens.

Three panels from the window of St. Vincent de Paul.

CHA
RI
TAS

S. VINCENT. DE. PAVL.

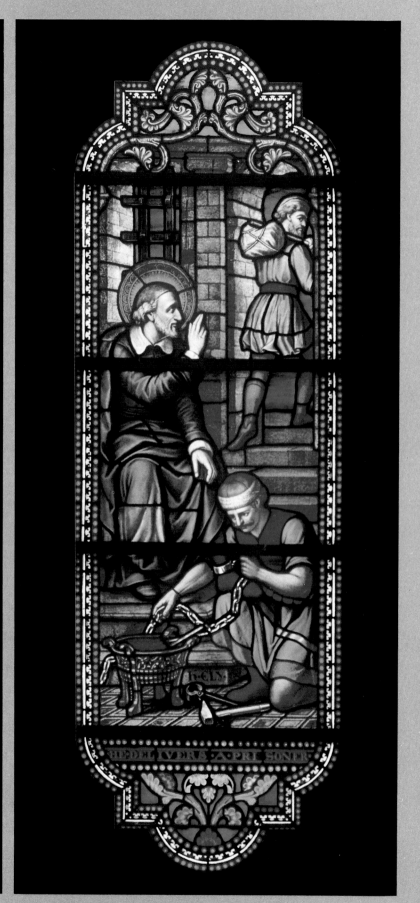

HE. DELIVERS. A. PRISONER

The chapel and altar of St. John the Evangelist was erected by Archbishop Corrigan as a memorial to his predecessors (four of whom were named John), and consecrated in 1894. The altar, of dark Siena marble, was designed by Renwick; the statue is of white Carrara. St. John holds a chalice out of which coils a snake — legend holds that once when John was given a cup containing poison, he made over it the sign of the cross and the poison came forth as a serpent.

The window above this chapel is dedicated to the Annunciation. The angel Gabriel announces his message of Christ to the Virgin Mary as, through a door partly concealed by a curtain, Joseph appears at work in his carpenter shop. The interior of the house at Nazareth is copied evidently from that of the Holy House of Loretto.

(Left) Chapel of St. Anthony of Padua, the most popular of the Sons of St. Francis. The figure in the foreground is of St. Anthony holding the Christ child. (Top) Altar and chapel of St. John the Evangelist, erected by Archbishop Corrigan as a memorial to his predecessors, four of whom bore the name John. The altar was designed by James Renwick.

Window of the Annunciation, south
wall of the cathedral.

The next alcove along the south aisle encloses the shrine of St. Elizabeth Ann Seton, canonized by Pope Paul VI in 1975 as "the first daughter of the United States of America to be glorified with the incomparable attribute" of sainthood.[3] The shrine to St. Elizabeth Seton, a native New Yorker, was created by the American sculptor Frederick Shrady and replaced an altar to the Polish Jesuit, St. Stanislaus Kostka. A bronze, free-standing statue to the saint portrays her holding a book in one hand, her other arm encircling the figure of a child. A curved screen, 7½ feet high and 20 feet long, forms a background for the statue and supports engravings of the three cities in which her religious calling took shape — New York, the Italian seaport of Livorno, and Emmitsburg, Maryland, where she established the first American religious community.

The window over the chapel is called St. Henry's window, after the eleventh-century Holy Roman Emperor. It shows him in a victorious battle scene.

Detail from the window of St. Henry.

Beyond the shrine to St. Elizabeth Seton is the chapel and altar of St. Rose of Lima, the first American saint to be canonized and the patroness of South America. The altar is adorned with selected Italian marbles and includes in the side niches statues of St. Catherine and St. Margaret.

The window above the chapel portrays the scene in Rome in 1854 when Pope Pius IX proclaimed the dogma of the Immaculate Conception, an event attended by Archbishop Hughes. The pope is depicted blessing the world and holding in his left hand the decree of that pronouncement. Above the gathering of cardinals, bishops, and religious, the figure of the Immaculate Conception is surrounded by the statues of St. Peter and St. Paul, replicas of the statues that stand at the entrance to St. Peter's in Rome.

Crossing the south transept, the visitor reaches the altar of the Blessed Sacrament, or the altar of the Sacred Heart, at which the sacrament is reserved in the tabernacle. A marble hexagon supports the tabernacle and a gold-leafed wooden baldachin hangs over it. In the center of the marble reredos of the altar is a statue of Christ as he appeared after the Resurrection.

91

The window over this altar at the clerestory level is devoted to the Sacred Heart. Christ is represented standing on the predella of an altar; before him stands St. Margaret Mary. An angel in the background has a scroll that reads, in French, "Behold the heart that loves men so much." To the left, over the south ambulatory aisle, is the window of St. Louis, King of France and last of the medieval crusaders. The scene shows the solemn procession in which the holy relics of the Crown of Thorns and a portion of the True Cross, given as a gift to St. Louis, were borne to their repository in the Sainte Chapelle in Paris.

The south aisle past the transept continues as the south ambulatory and leads first to the chapel and altar of St. Andrew, elder brother of St. Peter, one of the twelve apostles, and the first to be called by Christ. The statue shows the saint in a forceful pose, suggesting his vigorous life as a workman and missionary in Greece and the Balkan countries.

The window over this altar shows, in the center, St. Agnes, Virgin Martyr of Rome; the scene beneath her figure shows St. Agnes protected from her persecutor by an angel. To the left is St. Thomas; in the panels underneath, the doubting Thomas is assured by Christ that He is risen from the dead. The third figure, to the right, is St. James, brother of St. John; the scene below shows the Blessed Virgin appearing to James at Saragossa.

The altar of St. Theresa, the Little Flower, occupies the following alcove. The enframement of the altar is carved French limestone and fills the bay. Within the recess the walls are lined with Swiss cipolin marble. The altar and reredos are of white Italian marble, and in the reredos are fields of gold mosaic with ornamental inlays of roses in formally bordered panels. In the center of each is a carved symbol—on the left, the Veil of Veronica; on the right, the infant Christ in a field of passion flowers. The frontal of the altar is inscribed in gold mosaic: "The Blessed Theresa of the Infant Jesus — I will spend my heaven in doing good on earth." The marble figure of the saint, by the sculptor Mario Korbel, fills the center of the reredos under a marble canopy.

The window over the altar shows as the center figure St. Alphonsus Liguori vested as a bishop; the scene beneath represents him miraculously giving speech to a mute youth. The figure in the left division of the window is St. Theresa of Spain, founder of the Carmelite order of nuns; beneath it, the Lord appears to the saint shortly before her death. The third figure, to the right, represents St. Susanna; under the full-sized figure, an angel protects the saint from Maximian, a pagan whom her relative Emperor Diocletian wanted her to marry.

The Ambulatory

Continuing around the ambulatory, the archbishop's sacristy is just east of the altar of St. Theresa. The window in this bay depicts the death of St. Joseph, the earthly father of Christ. St. Joseph lies on a couch; Christ is seen seated at its foot and the Blessed Virgin is kneeling in prayer. Two angels hold a scroll that reads, "Blessed are the dead who die in the Lord."

statue of the *Pieta*, sculpted in 1906 b
William O. Partridge and styled afte
Michelangelo's masterpiece.

As the ambulatory approaches t
Lady chapel, the visitor passes on t
south side the chapel and altar of S
Elizabeth, designed — as were t
Lady chapel and the flanking chap
on its north side — by Charles
Matthews. In a high central nic
stands the statue of S Elizab
mother of St. John th Baptis
either side of the tabernacle door
panels that contain episodes from t
life of John the Baptist, and statuet
of the twelve apostles stand in nich
that form a retable, or altar sh
Outside the Lady chapel to the no
is the chapel of St. Michael and
Louis, displaying an elaborately
tailed marble altar. The reredos c
sists of three canopied niches—in t
left niche stands St. Louis of Fran
in the right, St. Michael the Arc
angel; the altar cross stands in the ce
tral niche. On the tabernacle door
bas-relief of Christ enthroned in
attitude of benediction Three shi
within the recessed panels of th
frontal show heraldic devices app
priate to the niches of the reredos

The Lady Chapel

*I*n keeping with the design of the great Gothic cathedrals of England and continental Europe, James Renwick had included in his original design a small chapel behind the main altar, in the middle of the apse. In the Middle Ages, this chapel, traditionally treated with an architecture more delicate and ornamental than that used throughout the rest of the building, was dedicated to the Virgin Mary and came to be known as the Chapel of Our Lady, or, more simply, the Lady Chapel. Situated close by the sanctuary, the most sacred part of the church, it was also used as the chapel of the Blessed Sacrament, and the Host was reserved in the tabernacle on the altar of the Lady Chapel. "From the churchly point of view as well as the architectural," wrote the *Times*, "it is the most important of all the chapels of a cathedral, so important that it is a separate and distinct edifice, not a chapel in the cathedral itself, but a building alongside of it, ranking ecclesiastically but just below it." In the Gothic cathedrals of Europe "in nearly every case these are exquisite pendants of the great main structure."[4]

St. Patrick's Lady chapel didn't get underway until after the turn of the century when a donation from the family of Eugene Kelly enabled work to begin — the structure was for some time popularly known as the "Kelly chapel." The cathedral organized a competition, and over a dozen architects from America, England, and France were invited to submit designs for the new chapel, including suggestions on how to remodel the flat eastern wall of the church. According to the rules of the competition, the drawings were to be unsigned and to have no mark or emblem that would identify their authors. The late Renwick's firm submitted a design, called by one critic a rather unimaginative imitation of the main cathedral. A French architect, ignoring the specifications entirely, continued his chapel across Madison Avenue. In reply to a letter reminding him of the public's right to the avenue, he said, with enviable aplomb, that the street might have to be changed. The anonymous drawings were judged by Archbishop Corrigan, a Columbia University professor of architecture, and the donor, each of whom picked the entry of Charles T. Matthews. His design led to the chapel as it appears today, facing east onto Madison Avenue and fitted neatly between the episcopal residence to the south and the rectory to the north. Construction was begun in 1901, and the first mass was said in the Lady chapel on Christmas, 1906.

The rear or east wall of the cathedral was removed and the side aisles running the length of the church were continued as an ambulatory leading behind the high altar. The rear of the ambulatory thus leads directly into the chapel, which is flanked by the two small, semioctagonal chapels, the altar of St. Michael and St. Louis, and the altar of St. Elizabeth. By this design the cathedral was lengthened and a graceful vista opened up running the length of the nave and extending behind the high altar into the airy confines of the chapel.

Behind the high altar of the cathedral proper a marble stairway leads to the sacristy underneath the chapel and to the burial crypt, which is separated by a

(Left) The altar of St. Michael and St. Louis, designed by Charles T. Mathews and built by Tiffany & Company. It was a gift of the Bouvier family, ancestors of Jacqueline Onassis.

(Below) Detail from a Lady chapel window: Monsignor Lavelle, longtime rector of St. Patrick's. (Right) Detail of Annunciation mosaic on front panel of the altar table.

bronze door. It will be recalled that in his original plan, Renwick indicated there would be no cellar or crypt—"the building rests on solid rock and the floor will be simply leveled off and covered with marble." And indeed the construction of the sacristy beneath the chapel was a delicate piece of engineering. The stairway to the sacristy passes beneath the foundations of the two rear piers of the cathedral, which support walls in the eastern end of the church. Solid rock had to be removed between these piers, and the slightest miscalculation in the blasting operations might have wrecked the entire cathedral. The construction work was successful, the foundations were judged to be in better condition even than they had been before work was begun, and the area under the chapel and the high altar now contains subcellars and utility rooms as well.

The Lady chapel, fifty-six feet long, twenty-eight feet wide, and fifty-six feet high, added almost 300 square yards of space to the cathedral. In design it is patterned on the thirteenth-century French Gothic style, though architectural critics say in parts it has the character and feeling of the more ornate design of a later century. It complements the cathedral in a delicate way, with sharper and less fantastic moldings and carvings, a more refined scale, an architecture on the whole more ornate and elaborate. An original feature in the treatment of the exterior is the small octagonal spire, decorated with open tracery, which is situated over each of the flanking chapels. The chapel is built of Vermont marble, and everything in the interior is stone, with the exception, as in the body of the cathedral itself, of the vaults, which are constructed of plaster. The chapel pavement is of polished marble inlaid in a gothic pattern; near the entrance, the heraldic arms of Pope Leo XIII are placed in mosaic.

Provision was made in the design for stained glass windows, and during the years 1927–1931 Paul Woodroffe, a graduate of the famous Jesuit School at Stonyhurst, England, designed and made the windows at his studio in Gloucestershire, after the style of the great cathedral at Chartres. The windows in the Lady chapel and the flanking chapels take as their subject the

fifteen mysteries of the Rosary of the Blessed Virgin; the glorious mysteries are illustrated in the Lady chapel itself, the joyful mysteries in the chapel to the left above the altar of St. Michael and St. Louis, the sorrowful mysteries in the chapel to the right above the altar of St. Elizabeth. The medallion at the top of each window depicts the mystery itself, while the lower parts of the window present the symbols, saints, prophets, or incidents pertinent to that particular mystery, the whole forming a kind of illustrated prayer on the life of Christ in relation to the Blessed Virgin. Dominant medallions include the coronation of our Lady in heaven, over the altar, and the Madonna and Child under a symbol of the Holy Spirit high in a lancet arch to the left.

Among the more fanciful portraits are those of St. Isaac Jogues, in a section of the lancet to the right of the Lady chapel altar, the priest murdered by the Iroquois in the seventeenth century—the saint, with his mutilated right hand visible, is preaching to an Indian who is pictured complete with colorful, if geographically inaccurate, feathered headdress and star-decorated teepee; Monsignor Lavelle, St. Patrick's famous rector, in a lancet on the right of the Lady chapel—a recognizable likeness, the monsignor is writing at his desk with a quill and by the light of a gas lamp; a Bolshevik, in the tower section of the first lancet on the right of the chapel, carrying a red flag and attacking with a sledgehammer the Christian cross atop a church.

The brilliant stained glass of the Lady chapel, predominantly blues—the color symbolic of the Virgin—and reds, relieved by whites, greens, and browns, lighted by the morning sun, has recalled for many the special beauty of Paris' Sainte Chapelle. From the church proper, behind the main altar, wrote *Architectural Record,* one sees "a mysterious maze of arches and columns and vaults, continuing the perspective beyond until it is lost in the dimness of the interior, through which at the end of the vista glow the mysteries of faith in flaming jewels of light."[5]

The altar was built and dedicated, by Archbishop Spellman, in 1942, and replaced an altar originally designed for another place in the church. Three steps of golden brown Siena marble lead to the mensa, or altar table, of Tavernelle marble, which displays a front panel richly inlaid in a mosaic design representing the Annunciation. The figures are surrounded by a rose vine, indicating the mystical rose which was "exalted like a cedar in Lebanon and as a rose plant in Jericho." The low reredos against which the table of the altar rests is of a cream-colored marble and shows a decorative inscription in Gothic lettering: the salutation of the Archangel Gabriel and the invocation of the Church. A white marble statue of the Virgin Mother, praying with outstretched arms, designed by Oronzio Maldarelli, grows out from and surmounts the reredos, and provides the focal point.

The chapel was finally completed in 1978, when a copper statue of the Virgin was put in position, according to the architect's plan, on the ridge of the roof overlooking the entrance on Madison Avenue. The statue, designed by Anthony Minervini, is eight feet in height and constructed of four-by-eight-foot sheets of copper welded together. The gently modeled figure crowns St. Patrick's Lady chapel, this most beckoning and well-loved location for weddings, special liturgies and devotions, and quiet meditation.

The North Aisle

Passing around the ambulatory and walking west toward the front of the cathedral, the visitor passes the usher's office on the right, an area that once contained a specially designed confessional for the use of deaf and mute penitents.

The window shows the nativity of Christ, with the Blessed Virgin offering her infant son for veneration.

The chapel and altar of St. Joseph shows the earthly father of Christ holding the child in his arms, a bronze statue positioned in a simple marble altar and under a canopy designed in the Renaissance style.

The window above the chapel is called the *Adoration of the Child Jesus* and illustrates scenes relating to the birth of Christ and the first Christmas. The shepherds and the Magi, the wise men of the East, are seen adoring the newborn Savior.

In the next alcove, the chancel organ, dedicated in 1927, is encased in an oak frame ornamented with Gothic elements of design and of symbolism. The console stands against the adjacent sanctuary pier.

The window illustrates the presentation of the Blessed Virgin Mary in the temple by her mother, St. Anne, and her father, St. Joachim, who comes forward with the high priest to receive the child.

The second transept altar, across the church from the altar of the Blessed Sacrament, is the altar of the Holy Family in the north transept, designed by Renwick in an elaborately Gothic treatment that befits its august dedication. Three scenes are carved in relief on the Caen stone reredos. The central composition shows the Holy Family; to the left is the Annunciation; on the panel to the right is the Adoration of the Magi. Figures and statuettes of angels surround the scenes, some standing within double niches that end in towering pinnacles.

The window of St. Monica and St. Augustine is seen high in the clerestory above the altar. St. Augustine stands by the deathbed of his mother, St. Monica, whose last injunction to him was: "My son, when I am dead lay this body anywhere, but remember me always at the Altar of God."

Detail from the St. Paul window.

The St. Paul window is seen to the right of the window of St. Augustine, over the north ambulatory aisle. The scene derives from the biblical passage in Acts 17, describing St. Paul preaching before the sages of the Areopagus, the place of the Greek high court near the Acropolis. On that occasion Paul said: "Men of Athens, I see that in every respect you are extremely religious. For as I was going about and observing objects of your worship, I found also an altar with this inscription: 'To the Unknown God.' What therefore you worship in ignorance, that I proclaim to you." St. Paul's most distinguished convert, who may be recognized in the scene, was Dionysius the Areopagite, who, according to tradition, is the St. Denis who founded the Church of Paris.

Passing through the north transept, the first alcove in the north aisle of the nave holds the chapel and altar of the Holy Relics, formerly called the chapel of St. Veronica. Precious relics received through the years by the archbishops of New York are kept here for public veneration and are described in an inscription at the altar rail. The altar is of Carrara marble and Mexican onyx; a mosaic of the Holy Face adorns the reredos.

St. Bernard's window is situated over the chapel. Dressed in the white robe of the Cistercian order, the great abbot and doctor stands in the central division. He preaches the Second Crusade in twelfth-century France, as a mother and a child, cardinals, bishops, monks, and crusaders with flying banners listen.

The shrine of St. John Neumann replaced a chapel dedicated to St. Augustine. Ordained in old St. Patrick's Cathedral, the saint did missionary work in western New York State and was consecrated bishop of Philadelphia in 1852. He was elevated to sainthood in 1977. The shrine shows a rough-hewn statue of St. John Neumann seated facing two children and before a curving wall of irregular stone blocks holding a metal figure of old St. Patrick's Cathedral. Symbolic carvings in the shrine represent significant events in the saint's life: the monstrance, indicating the forty hours devotion he established on a diocesan basis; the tree, symbolizing his missionary work; the women religious, signifying his founding of the Sisters of the Third Order of St. Francis.

The window above the chapel depicts the martyrdom of St. Lawrence, showing the famous deacon, one of the seven of the Roman Church, stretched on a gridiron. A glowing fire blazes beneath him. St. Lawrence's Acts report that "his face appeared to be surrounded with an extraordinary light, and his broiled body to exhale a sweet, agreeable smell."

aptiste de la Salle, founder of the
stitute of the Brothers of the
hristian Schools and a pioneer of
odern education. The altar is re-
ete with sculptural panels and
gures, notably a large statue of the
int in the central niche. In the panel
its left a carved scene represents his
ve of charity and almsgiving; in the
nel to the right he is shown
structing little boys. The frontal of
e altar depicts the scene of his
ath.

The window above the chapel
ows Pope Benedict XIII giving his
pprobation to the constitution of the
rothers of the Christian Schools and
ceiving Brother Timothy, the su-
rior general of the institute. The
ight uniforms of the Swiss Guards
d others of the papal court contrast
ith the dark habits of the brothers
tending the scene.

The chapel and altar of St. Brigid
d St. Bernard is designed around
plicas of famous Celtic works of art.
niches to the left and right of the
redos are St. Brigid, friend of St.
atrick and patroness of Ireland, and
. Bernard of Clairvaux.

The window above the chapel
lates an episode in the life of the
ish missionary St. Columbanus,
ho built an abbey at Luxeuil near the
alace of the Burgundian king
hierry III. The saint is shown here
jecting the king's gift and rebuking
im for his scandalous life.

Chapel and altar of St. Jean Baptiste de la Salle.

The bapistry encloses the eight-sided font of Bottoccino marble, carved with an inscription and traditional baptismal symbols, such as the *Agnus Dei* ("Lamb of God"). The spire-shaped cover of the font is carved of oak.

The window represents the three baptisms as described in theology: the baptism of water, the baptism of blood by martyrdom, and the baptism of desire when no one is near to administer the Sacrament and the soul ardently desires it. In the central lancet, Christ is baptized by John in the River Jordan. To the left is the scene representing the baptism of desire; to the right is the baptism of martyrdom. Symbols of God the Father, the Son, and the Holy Spirit are seen in the tracery above.

This window contains a curious mistake, unnoticed until recently. The small panel of lettered stained glass immediately beneath the feet of Christ is set in backwards and upside down, to read "BAPT O-WSI F-OUR - LORD" instead of "BAPT ISM-O F-OUR - LORD."

Chapel and altar of St. Brigid and St. Bernard.

The Transepts

Set into niches and recessed panels in the walls of the transepts are marble statues of the doctors of the church, as some of the great ecclesiastical teachers and theologians are called, and the famous sculptures of the stations of the cross. In the south side, seated in the lower niches are statues of St. Anselm, St. Bernard, St. Bonaventure, and St. Alphonsus Liguori; in the upper enclosures are St. Gregory the Great, St. Francis de Sales, St. Ambrose, and St. Jerome. An identical wall arrangement in the north transept shows, seated in the lower niches, the four great doctors of the Eastern Church: St. John Chrysostom, St. Basil the Great, St. Gregory of Nazianzen, and St. Athanasius. St. Dominic stands in the upper tier, to the left of the door, and St. Thomas Aquinas is to the right.

The sculptures in panels recessed in three walls of the south transept and in two walls of the north depict the stations of the cross, or the successive stages of Christ's journey to his crucifixion on Mount Calvary. Traditionally, a prescribed order of worship is followed for each station, a form of devotion that developed in the late Middle Ages when the Holy Land, which had been conquered by the Turks, was inaccessible to Christian pilgrims—the scenes of Christ's passion and death were represented by crosses or pictures set up in a church or, sometimes, on the road to it. The sculptures in St. Patrick's were designed in Holland by Peter J. H. Cuypers, a celebrated ecclesiastical artist. They were carved in the Stolzenberg ateliers in Roermond, Holland, of cream-colored Caen stone. When the first three arrived in the United States in April 1893, they were sent immediately to the Chicago World's Fair, where they won prizes for the Dutch exhibit. The seven stations in the south transept begin, at the left, near the Sacred Heart altar, with station i: Jesus is condemned to death; and follow ii: Jesus is made to bear his cross; iii: Jesus falls the first time; iv: Jesus meets his afflicted mother; v: Jesus is assisted by the Cyrenean; vi: Veronica presents the towel to Jesus; vii: Jesus falls the second time. The stations continue in the north transept, beginning at the east wall, viii: Jesus speaks to the daughters of Jerusalem; ix: Jesus falls the third time; x: Jesus is stripped of his garments; xi: Jesus is nailed to the cross; xii: Jesus dies on the cross; xiii: Jesus is taken down from the cross; xiv: Jesus is laid in the tomb. The Gothic tracery over each station shows a decorative cross incorporating a wooden cross, the official mark of the station.

(Above) Station of the cross vii: Jesus falls the second time. (Below right) Three stations of the cross located in the south transept—ix: Jesus falls the third time; x: Jesus is stripped of his garments; xi: Jesus is nailed to the cross.

The Windows

Certainly, the windows of St. Patrick's are a stellar attraction. There are seventy in all, most made in France near the cathedral town of Chartres. At varying levels, shining through the light of early morning or of the evening sun, the stained-glass panels set in the walls of the church are alternately glittering and jewellike or softly glowing in dusky shades of blue and rose. The windows crowning the small chapels and altars and those illuminating the Lady chapel, previously described, invite the visitor to close inspection. Among the remaining windows, those at the four points of the cross — at the west end, the apse, and the north and south transepts — are supreme.

High over the bronze doors in the Fifth Avenue wall and visible from the nave above the great organ is the famous rose window, twenty-six feet in diameter and filled with stained glass in geometric patterns designed by the Morgan Brothers firm of New York. Also known as the wheel window, the circular window can be traced back to Roman times; it became a decorative form in Byzantine and Romanesque building, and is perhaps the best-known feature of Gothic design.

Down the long nave of the cathedral, the rose window faces the high altar and the eleven surrounding windows of the sanctuary, including the five windows of the polygonal apse. The six remaining are called the windows of the sacrifice; five represent the sacrifices of the Old Testament that prefigured the great one of the New Testament, the sacrifice on Calvary, which is the subject of the sixth window.

Facing the altar, the first window to be seen on the north side of the sanctuary (above the archbishop's throne) represents the sacrifice of Abel. In the foreground, the two sons of Adam each tend an altar. On the altar tended by Abel, a lamb is being consumed; the smoke ascends between the youth's extended arms and forms a cloud, on which rests a figure of the Holy Father. On the left, the figure of Cain is seen crouching; from his altar the smoke ascends ungracefully and forms a cloud from which emerges a horned figure of Lucifer.

The second window on the same side shows the sacrifice of Noe. The patriarch and his family offer sacrifice to God in thanksgiving for their deliverance. A lamb burns on the altar, and in the foreground are a sacrificial knife, vessels of blood, and slain beasts and fowl ready to be consumed. In the background, oxen, asses, and deer are browsing on a hillside; Mount Ararat rises in the distance, the ark resting on its summit and flocks of birds circling the peak. A shining rainbow encloses the scene.

The third window represents the sacrifice of Melchisedech. According to the biblical passage: "Melchisedech, the King of Salem, bringing forth bread and wine, for he was the priest of the most high God, blessed Abram, and said — Blessed be Abram by the most high God, who created heaven and earth." In the foreground, Melchisedech holds a smoking censer near the offering of bread and wine before him. Around him stand Abram and a group of armed warriors, just returned from victory. In the tracery above this scene an angel keeps watch, and around the circle that encloses it is the legend in Latin: "Thou art a priest forever according to the order of Melchisedech."

The Sacrifice of Abel.

JOHN·JOHNSTON

The first window on the south side of the sanctuary shows the sacrifice of Abraham. Abraham, Isaac, and the angel fill the foreground, which shows Abraham preparing to sacrifice his son, who rests, with bound hands, on a crude altar of wood. With one hand the angel gently restrains Abraham's stroke of the sword and with the other points to "a ram amongst the briars, sticking fast by the horns." In the background is a mountain scene in "the land of vision."

The next window illustrates the eating of the paschal lamb. In a Hebrew household in Egypt it is the night of the institution of the feast of the Passover. The father of the family prays, joined by other members who stand around the board, their loins girt, shoes on their feet, and holding staves in their hands, while a slave brings in the roasted paschal lamb. At the door a woman sprinkles the doorway with "a bunch of hyssop, steeped in the blood of the lamb, that he who destroyed the first-born might not touch them." Against the dark night sky, the destroying angel goes about his deadly errand.

The final sanctuary window represents the great sacrifice of Calvary. The Mount of Calvary rises in the distance, three naked crosses silhouetted against the sky. Christ has been laid in the tomb. An allegorical figure of Error is seen fleeing into the night, surrounded by owls and bats and the emblems of darkness, and stumbling over the debris of broken altars and implements of pagan worship. In the foreground is an allegorical figure of Truth, who, with uplifted cross, rules the world. Before it kneels the figure of Cardinal McCloskey, placing on the altar as an offering to Truth the new St. Patrick's Cathedral. The window bears an inscription commemorating the date of his consecration as cardinal, 15 March 1875.

The Sacrifice of Noe.

The five apsidal windows above the high altar were installed in 1941, at the time the new altar was put in place. The windows were designed by and made in the studio of Charles J. Connick of Boston, under the supervision of the architects Maginnis and Walsh. Each window is composed of two lancet divisions with tracery at the top and contains six medallions grouped in parallel pairs. Together, the medallions illustrate thirty parables of Christ, and below the medallions are distinctive symbols of the Evangelists whose Gospels record these parables. The three larger members of the tracery at the head of the windows carry symbols of the seven sacraments. In the smaller members of the tracery are stars and flames, symbolic of steadfastness and zeal.

The central window illustrates Christ as head of the kingdom of God. In the trefoils of its tracery kneeling angels bear symbols of the Holy Eucharist: the chalice, the monstrance, and the crucifix. The medallions, from left to right and top to bottom, tell the stories of the prodigal son, the lost sheep, the sower, the lost coin, the great supper, and the good samaritan.

The window to the left of center, and the one to the extreme left, present parables concerned with the origin of Christ's kingdom. Figures in the tracery bear symbols related to the baptismal symbols of God the Father, Son, and Holy Ghost — the hand from the clouds, the *Agnus Dei*, and the descending dove. The medallions illustrate the parables of the laborers, the wedding garment, the wicked or ungrateful husbandmen, the sheep and the goats, the two sons, and the rich fool.

The window at the extreme left carries symbols of the sacraments of matrimony and holy orders. In the tracery are the insignia of the bishop's miter, the maniple of the priesthood, and the seven crosses of minor orders. The clasped hands and cross symbolize the sacrament of matrimony. The lancet medallions recall the parables of the leaven, the mustard seed, the hidden treasure, the pearl of great price, the net cast into the sea, and the cockle or tares among the good seed.

The two windows to the right of center tell stories related to the members of the kingdom of God and their duties. The tracery at the top of the first of these windows shows the symbols for contrition — the heart pierced with arrows; for confession — the scales and keys; and for satisfaction — the scourge, all related to the sacrament of repentance. The medallions tell the parables of the Pharisee and the publican, Dives and Lazarus, the unjust steward, the ten virgins, the five talents, and the unmerciful servant.

The fifth window is devoted to the sacraments of the Holy Spirit — confirmation and extreme unction. In the tracery are symbols of the descending dove bearing the sacred characters, *Chi Rho*, the monogram of Christ; the miter and shield inscribed with the cross stand for confirmation, and the ampulla for the holy oils, with the letters *O.I.* on it, are representative of extreme unction. The parables of the medallions are the barren fig tree, the lilies of the field, the raw cloth on the old garment, new wine in old bottles, the candle under a bushel, and the fig tree blossoming.

Over the south and north transept doors the great storied windows of the cathedral dedicated to St. Patrick and to the Virgin Mary, respectively, fill the space to the very top of the gable. Each window is twenty-eight feet wide by fifty-eight feet high, and divided into six lancet divisions, in which a series of scenes tells the story of its subject's life, a sort of epic in stained glass.

The detail at left shows the scene from his life called "He is taken prisoner at the age of thirteen."

The titular window of the cathedral, St. Patrick's window over the Fiftieth Street entrance, is one of two devoted to the saint and gives his history in eighteen scenes. Beginning at the base of the left-hand bay and reading the scenes upward in lines of three each, the story unfolds as follows: St. Patrick is baptzied; he is kidnapped and taken prisoner at the age of thirteen; an angel reveals to him his vocation; he preaches the Gospel on board a ship carrying him back to his homeland; he is sold to King Milcho; he is set free at Maestric; he is made a cleric by his uncle, St. Martin, Bishop of Tours; he studies on the island of Lerins; he is ordained a priest by Bishop Sancaur; he sails for Rome; he receives the blessing of Pope Celestine; he is consecrated bishop by St. Amataur; he visits St. Germain d'Auxerre; he converts Dichu and his family on his arrival in Ireland; he gives Holy Communion to the princesses Ethna and Fethlema; he raises Malfric from the dead; St. Patrick dies; and the angels sing his funeral dirge. Above the medallions the scene in the center of the tracery shows the saint's coronation in heaven; circled around it hover angels, copied after Fra Angelico, each holding a scroll on which is written one line of a hymn to the glories of heaven.

St. Patrick's window was made in the ateliers of Henry Ely in Nantes, France, and was the gift of the old St. Patrick's to the new. Accurate in perspective, this remarkable "true" painting in stained glass is seen to best advantage in the light of early evening.

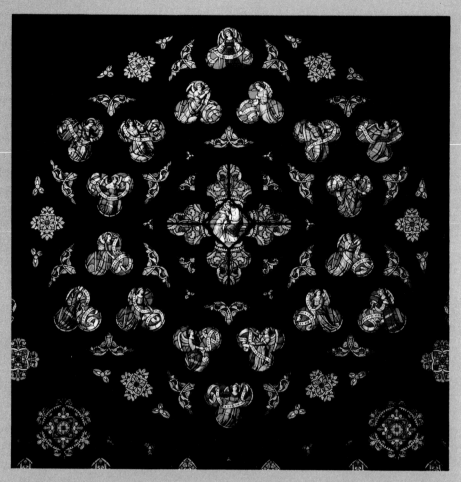

The window of the Blessed Virgin over the north transept door at Fifty-first Street corresponds in design to St. Patrick's window, and tells the story of the life, death, assumption, and coronation of the Mother of Christ. Beginning at the lower left-hand corner, the story proceeds: the Virgin Mary is born; she is presented in the temple; she is taught by her mother, St. Anne; Mary is espoused to St. Joseph; she hears the message of the Annunciation; the angel appears to St. Joseph in his sleep; the Virgin Mary visits St. Elizabeth; the baby Jesus is born; the shepherds adore the infant in Mary's arms; Jesus is worshiped by the Magi; Jesus is presented in the temple; the flight into Egypt begins; Joseph carries Jesus during the journey; the Holy Family is at Nazareth; Mary is the Mother of Sorrows; the Holy Spirit descends upon Mary and the apostles; the Virgin Mary dies; and she is brought to heaven.

High above, in the center of the tracery, the coronation scene shows Mary receiving the crown from her son, while the Holy Ghost in the form of a dove and God the Father look down. Around the coronation scene the design is filled with the symbols of Mary's various titles.

The window of the Blessed Virgin was made in the ateliers of Nicholas Lorin of Chartres, France, and was the gift of the diocese of Albany, whose cathedral was built and dedicated to the Virgin Mary by Cardinal McCloskey when he was the first bishop of Albany.

The second St. Patrick's window is set into the west wall of the south transept and is similar in size to the windows over the side chapels. It was James Renwick's gift to the cathedral, and the architect himself plays a part in the stained-glass scene. St. Patrick appears in the upper portion dressed as a bishop, the apostle of Ireland, preaching to an assembly of people. In the distance workmen build a primitive church. The lower three panels show Renwick submitting his cathedral plan to Archbishop Hughes, who is seated at a table. Cardinal McCloskey stands in the foreground holding the part of the building that he altered from the original plan, and near the archbishop are Reverend John M. Farley; Nicholas Lorin, craftsman of the window; several religious; and an apprentice architect unfolding a roll of drawings. A portfolio against the table reads "James Renwick, Esq., New York," and the window is dated 1879.

The corresponding window on the north side of the church, set in the west wall of that transept, is the window of St. Charles Borromeo. The cardinal, bearing a crucifix, walks in solemn procession from the door of the cathedral of Milan. Before him lie two victims of the plague, a mother and her clinging child. Below, a dissolute monk attacks the cardinal, who is conducting evening prayer in his private chapel.

FROM JAMES RENWICK·

Four transept windows are dedicated to the Evangelists, Matthew, Mark, Luke, and John. All are on the same level, designed on the same pattern, and of the same size as the windows of the wide chapel. They were made by M. Ely of Nantes, France. On the east side of the north transept door St. Matthew's window shows a life-size figure of the saint, a pen in one hand and a book of his Gospel in the other. Beneath him is the distinctive symbol of St. Matthew, the figure of an angel. The two side bays around the figure depict scenes from Matthew's life: his vocation, in which Christ says to him, "Follow me"; St. Matthew preaching the Gospel in Ethiopia; raising the king's son from the dead; the saint's martyrdom.

St. Mark's window, on the west side of the same door, shows the Evangelist with pen and book, the winged lion that is his symbol lying at his feet. The four scenes from his life fill the side bays: writing the gospel with St. Peter; building the church of St. Peter, Alexandria; Christ appearing to St. Mark in prison; his martyrdom.

In the south transept, on the west side of the entrance, is St. Luke's window. The Evangelist's figure is seen above his emblem, the ox. In the side bays, Luke is writing his Gospel in company with St. Paul; he preaches in the Thebaid; he paints the portrait of the Virgin Mary; his martyrdom.

This page: Detail from window of St. Matthew, the center panel. Facing page: A side panel of the window of St. Mark — writing the Gospel with St. Peter.

126

St. John's window occupies the corresponding position on the east side of the door. St. John's emblem, the eagle, perches at his feet. The four scenes in the remaining bays show John reposing on the bosom of Christ; John, in company with St. Peter, curing the cripple at the gate of the temple, saying "In the name of Jesus, arise and walk"; converting the young man who had become an outlaw; writing his Apocalypse.

The High Altar and Baldachin

The focal point of the cathedral, the place of sacrifice and the table of Holy Communion, is a simple altar of Italian marble with a bronze crucifix and the bark of Peter, symbol of the Church, on the frontal. Surrounding it and rising majestically toward the vaulted ceiling of the sanctuary is the great baldachin, or canopy, the most arresting architectural detail inside the cathedral and the element that first catches the eye of any entering its doors. The high altar and its baldachin are a relatively new addition to the building.

With plans for the completion of the Lady chapel in hand, cathedral architects studied the original main altar, an imposing mass of reredos that effectively masked the flat wall somewhat exigently constructed pending addition of the chapel behind it. James Renwick did not know when or, indeed, if the chapel would ever be built, and he designed the elaborate main altar to disguise the truncated plan. Although the chapel was completed in 1906, it was not until 1942 that a high altar appropriate to the new, elongated design was added. The old altar was dismantled, to be relocated at Fordham University in the Collegiate chapel, and replaced by the present structure, which was designed, again, by the architectural firm of Maginnis and Walsh.

Made entirely of bronze, which glows with a sheen golden enough to make children gasp, the baldachin rises to a height of fifty-seven feet above the sanctuary floor. Its four supporting pillars are crowned with highly decorated arches, which in turn support a gabled roof with a slender steeplelike flèche. The entire structure is worked with intricate detail that is simultaneously spectacular and correct. Throughout, the elements of the decoration, when studied as a whole, tell the story of the Redemption of Mankind. Figures of saints set in the front and rear of the canopy amplify the theme, as do the crowning figures that occupy the upper gables. Two classes of decoration are used. The first consists principally of statues of God, angels, patriarchs, prophets, apostles, and saints. Nine statuettes in niches on the rear of the baldachin are devoted chiefly to Old Testament figures; an equal number on the front relate to the New Testament. The second type of decorative elements is the colored shields. Found on the arches of the altar canopy, they bear symbols on them complementing the significance of the statues of Christ. Within the baldachin twelve more shields in white and gold carry emblems relating to the passion, death, and resurrection of Jesus. The colored shields on both sides of the structure are concerned in their design with the Mass. The description of the theme begins at the rear of the baldachin.

1. St. Michael. The Archangel stands at the very top of the structure. He faces the congregation from a pedestal set upon a floral finial of the spire, which rises from the flèche, or spire on the roof of the baldachin. St. Michael, in Catholic tradition and liturgy, is the champion and protector of the Church. He is one of the three angels mentioned by name in the Bible. The other two are Raphael and Gabriel. In the statue he wears a short tunic with low ornamented collar. His feet are greaved; a sword hangs by his side; in his

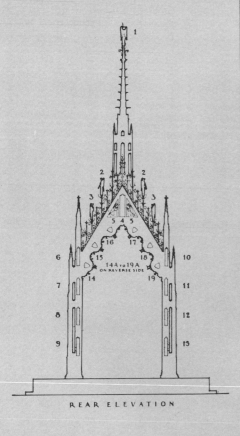

REAR ELEVATION

right hand he holds a jewelled crown, ornate with *fleur de lis* and topped with a globe and cross. The long staff he holds in his left hand terminates in a cross.

2. Herald angels. These statues are also free standing on pedestals on the floral cresting of the gables. There are four, two on the front and two on the rear, and they hold long trumpets, which they are in the act of blowing as they face the north and the south.

3. Adoring angels. These four statues are located on the cresting below the herald angels and slightly below the central niches over each arch, wherein are statues of Christ. They stand with hands clasped at their breast in the act of adoring Him as the teacher, on the rear, and as Christ the King, on the front elevation.

4. The Messiah, the gentle teacher. The central decorative object that dominates the rear of the baldachin is a richly ornate niche sheltering a statue of Jesus. He appears in the attitude of supreme teacher of the human race. Located above the arch, with its rich tracery canopy at the apex of the pediment, the statue is attired in a simple flowing tunic. His right hand is at his breast; in his left hand he holds a book.

5. In the spandrels, each side of the central niche, are two kneeling angels.

Eight statuettes are located in niches that are an integral part of the two piers of the baldachin. Beginning at the top, the four on the pier at the Epistle, or south, side are Melchisedech, Abraham, Moses, and David.

6. Melchisedech. King of Salem, contemporary of Abraham, offered to God a sacrifice of bread and wine. In the statue, Melchisedech wears a high, plain crownlike headdress. His beard is broad and oriental. His hands, breaking through the folds of his mantle, grasp to his breast a large chalice.

7. Abraham. Patriarch, father of all believers, and progenitor of the Hebrew nation, Abraham received from God the promise that in his seed all peoples should be blessed. He lived probably in the nineteenth or twentieth century before Christ. He was the father of Isaac and grandfather of Jacob. Because of his faith and obedience to God he was ready to sacrifice his only son. In the statuette, Abraham, with long beard, broad hat, and long mantle gown, looks toward heaven while he holds a knife above the head of Isaac. With hands bound and clasped behind him and standing on the head of a ram protruding from beneath the feet of Abraham, the innocent Isaac looks up to his father.

8. Moses. Patriarch, Hebrew leader, and lawgiver, Moses received on Mount Sinai God's written law, the Decalogue, or Ten Commandments. He lived in the twelfth century before Christ. The statuette depicts the Great Patriarch as he was in the desert, holding in his hands the brazen serpent twined around a staff formed here into a cross. At his feet in symbolic miniature is an ox in allusion to the sacrifice of the Hebrews.

9. David. David was a prophet and king of Israel. The greater part of the book of Psalms was composed by David, "the sweet singer of God." As prophet he clearly foretells the divinity, priesthood, resurrection, ascension, and everlasting reign of the Messiah. The statuette shows David wearing a low crown ornamented with the emblem called the Star of David. As the elderly

and humbled king he holds the crown of thorns, symbolic here of Christ's passion, which David prophesied in Psalms 21 and 68. The partly unrolled scroll and the harp shown embroidered on the border of his long gown declare David's office of royal psalmist.

The four statuettes on the pier at the Gospel, or north, side of the rear are Isaias, Holy Simeon, St. John the Baptist, and St. Peter.

10. Isaias. He is the first and greatest of the four major prophets (including Jeremias, Ezechiel, and Daniel). According to Hebraic tradition, he was of the royal blood of the kings of Juda and died a martyr seven centuries before Christ's birth. The Book of the Prophecy of Isaias foretells the miraculous virginity of Christ's mother. He carries a scroll on which is written in Latin: *Ecce Virgo Concipiet* ("Behold, a virgin shall conceive"). Alongside Isaias' scroll is a branch, the root of Jesse, symbolic of Mary.

11. Holy Simeon. This "just and devout" man of Jerusalem greeted the infant Savior on his presentation in the temple. In the statuette the elderly Simeon holds the infant Jesus in his arms.

12. St. John the Baptist. St. John preached penance, lived as a hermit in the desert, predicted that the kingdom of God was at hand, and fulfilled the prophecy of Isaias 40:3: "I am the voice of one crying in the wilderness: Make ready the way of the Lord." In the statuette he wears a garment of camel's hair and the loose fold of a mantle. He holds to his breast a small lamb and with his left hand a scroll on which is written: *Ecce Agnus Dei* ("Behold the Lamb of God"), the words St. John the Baptist used in his prophetic greeting to Christ.

13. St. Peter. The fisherman of Galilee was chief of the apostles, head and supreme pastor of Christ's church. St. Peter here appears as chief of the apostles, wearing a simple tunic and a mantle over one shoulder, against the folds of which he holds with his right hand a scroll in which is written: *Tu Es Petrus* ("Thou art Peter"). His left hand clasps two keys, symbols of his office as vicar of Christ on earth—symbols, too, of the episcopal power that resides in the pope.

The six polychromed shields on the rear arch of the baldachin complement in their symbolic designs the significance of the eight statuettes. If one were to stand facing the back of the altar and read clockwise, they would be seen as follows:

14. The first shield has a purple background; a triple flaming red sword placed vertically is crossed by a gold trumpet. These symbols are emblematic of the defense of the Israelites preserving their spiritual heritage during the epochs when they left Egypt and when Josue was their leader.

15. On the next shield is a floral design (the one opposite it is similar). It is a white shield with three green oak leaves, two gold acorns, below which is an ivy leaf. These are significant of the Hebraic strength and tenacity to the promise of the Messiah.

16. The upper shield, of blue field, carries an open star; the interwoven design is of Celtic character and was called the Hand of God; within the gold

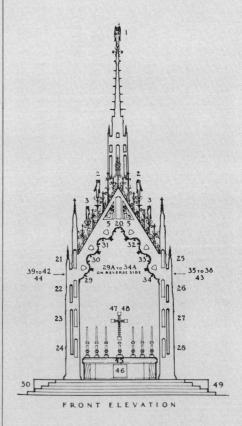

FRONT ELEVATION

star is the white letter *M* meaning Mary, through whom would come Christ. Below the star is a rainbow.of the six primary colors, the sign God gave to Noe as a covenant between God and the earth.

17. At the right side of the arch is the next shield, of green field, on which are two white tablets of the Mosaic law with the Ten Commandments denoted by red Roman numerals. They symbolize the law given to Moses on Mount Sinai.

18. The next shield, at the center, is of white field and composed of a vertical branch of yellow palm and green olive leaves. Both are symbolic of triumph and peace, recalling also that a dove brought to Noe an olive twig when the flood subsided. On Palm Sunday the liturgy of the Church commemorates Christ's triumphant entry into Jerusalem with the blessing of palms.

19. With a red field, the last shield on the rear of the baldachin is composed of a gold cross, a circle at its center. Attached to the upper arm of the cross is a silver yoke, which gives balance to silver scales held by green cords. By this cross of Redemption, the Messiah undid the effects of the Fall, restored peace and justice, reconciled man with God, and established grace and the Sacraments.

Turning to the main arch, which faces the sanctuary and the congregation, the arrangement of the iconography of the front elevation follows the same order as that of the rear elevation. This division of the general theme of the Redemption is devoted to the New Testament.

20. Christ as king and high priest. The statue is in the central niche, which dominates the elevation at the apex of the pediment. Christ wears a crown and is vested in the apparel of his priestly and royal office. The alb has a border on which is an orphrey ornamented with two angels holding a crown above a tabernacle; the maniple is on his left arm; the chasuble is of Gothic design; He wears also an imperial ermine cape, and over all these vestments is the long pallium. His hands show the wounds of his crucifixion and are in the position of one receiving acts of worship.

On the two front piers of the baldachin below the figure of Christ the King stand eight statuettes in richly designed niches. They are saints chosen as exemplars and defenders of Christ's life, teachings, and the life of his church. The following four are on the Gospel side:

21. St. Athanasius. He was confessor, bishop, patriarch of Alexandria in Egypt, where he died in AD 373, and one of the four doctors of the Eastern Church. In the statuette St. Athanasius is portrayed as the theologian, the defender of the integrity of the Catholic creed. Both hands hold a long scroll in which is a traditional symbol of the Holy Trinity.

22. St. John Chrysostom. Confessor, bishop of Constantinople, doctor of the Church, he was called Chrysostom, the "golden tongued," because of the marvelous and persuasive power of his eloquence, which swayed the whole Eastern Empire. He is here visualized as the preacher, the greatest ever heard in a Christian pulpit. He is attired in his priestly robes with the pallium and the stole conspicuous. He holds the open book in tribute to his masterly

commentaries on the Sacred Scriptures.

23. St. Ambrose. St. Ambrose was confessor, bishop of Milan in the years 374–397, doctor of the Church, statesman, and administrator. In the statuette he is vested in the dress of his episcopal office, the perfect model of a Christian bishop, the guardian of his flock. He holds a book to recall that one of his most important writings constitutes a manual of Christian morality. In his right hand is a scourge and there is a beehive at his feet, the one symbolic of his asceticism, the other of his industry.

24. St. Augustine of Hippo. He was born in 354, died in 430, confessor, bishop, and the greatest of the doctors of the Catholic world. St. Augustine appears as the great thinker and lover of Christ. His mantle is covered with a hood to recall that he also introduced religious poverty and community life into his residence, which became the nursery of African monasteries and bishops. In his right hand he holds two books symbolic of his learning and on the scroll held up by his left hand is carved, *Tolle lege* ("Take and read"), words that, referring to the Scriptures, he heard in the garden in Milan. At his feet is the bishop's miter, the two peaks of which symbolize the love of God and of one's neighbor, as well as the Old and the New Testament. The miter is also called the helmet of salvation.

The next four statuettes are on the right side of the altar, or the Epistle side.

25. St. Benedict. This son of a Roman noble was founder of the Benedictine order. St. Benedict is dressed in the habit of his order: the monk's cowl, the cappa, scapular, and tunic, or monastic gown. The volume he holds open stands for his great rule, and the bird resting on this book is the raven he fed daily.

26. St. Dominic. He was founder of the Order of Preaching Friars, usually called the Dominicans. In the statuette, the saint is dressed in the habit of his order. The emblem on his forehead recalls an incident that occurred at his baptism when a star is said to have settled on his infant brow. At his feet, the dog with a torch in its mouth commemorates the prophetic dream of St. Dominic's mother before his birth. In his hands is held an open book, symbolic of his learning and indicating also that preaching the Gospel and teaching constitute the chief occupation of the followers of St. Dominic. The lily in blossom and branch shaped in low relief upon his tunic pays symbolic tribute to his cultivation of a greater devotion to the Virgin Mary.

27. St. Francis of Assisi. Confessor, founder of the order of Friars Minor (usually called the Franciscans), he was born at Assisi, Italy, in 1182 and died there in 1226. Son of a wealthy cloth merchant, he abandoned all to preach penance and brotherly love and became the "Poor Man of Assisi" for the love of God. Here St. Francis' sweet austerity and sanctity are conspicuous. His habit is simple, with small hood, the knotted cord, and sandals. The two doves and an olive branch he holds in his pierced hands exemplify his gentleness and love of all God's creatures, and are reminiscent of his preaching to the birds, an incident in his life made famous by Giotto's painting.

28. St. Ignatius Loyola. Confessor, founder and first general of the Jesuits, he was born in 1491 in his father's castle in northern Spain and died in Rome in

1556. St. Ignatius here wears the simple cassock and the clerical cap, called the *biretta*, in the habit of the diocesan clergy. In his left hand is a small cross with three divisions. This form is called the papal cross and connotes the services the Jesuits rendered to the pope. The book in his right hand acknowledges the saint's religious work, called the *Spiritual Exercises*, and on its cover is written the Jesuit motto: *Ad Majorem Dei Gloriam*, "To the greater glory of God."

The six polychromed shields on the front elevation bear symbols relating to the life of Christ. They are described in clockwise order.

29. On a red shield a white dolphin looks at a small gold cross backed by a smaller silver ring. The dolphin or the fish is an ancient Christian symbol of Jesus. Its significance here is based on the acrostic formed by the letters of the Greek word for fish, *I-Ch-Th-U-S*,—in English, "Jesus Christ, Son of God, Saviour." The early Christians placed this dolphin symbol in the catacombs, and it betokened to them the significance of the Holy Eucharist.

30. The next shield is blue and its floral design is the red passion flower with five golden pistils and two green leaves below the blossom. This flower is employed in symbolic reference to Christ's passion and death.

31. The top shield at the left has on its green background a closed crown of gold; the open sectors of it are red, the jewels are silver, and it is surmounted by a gold cross encompassed by a silver circle. The crown is emblematic of peace and union with God.

32. On a blue field, the next shield, uppermost at the right side of the arch, carries a gold trefoil design of Celtic origin; red flames in triple division are set at the three depressions of the triangular design. This is a symbol of the Most Holy Trinity, central doctrine of the Christian religion.

33. The center shield at the right is red with a floral design composed of a double mystical white rose without thorns; the heart is golden, the leaves are green. The rose is a symbol of love and purity.

34. The final shield on this front arch bears a gold Latin cross on a green field; left and right behind the cross are two silver keys, symbolizing the death of Christ and the victory that opened heaven to all who die believing in God.

The third series of twelve shields is on the interior of the baldachin arches, grouped intimately about the altar. Their designs are related to the last days of Christ, which the Church commemorates on Holy Thursday, Good Friday, and Easter Sunday. These twelve shields have all-white enamel fields with gold symbolic designs. The first six are to be viewed as one stands at the altar and faces Fifth Avenue. Reading clockwise, the first three recall the events of the Last Supper, the second three those of the Garden of Gethsemane and in Pilate's court.

34A. The first shield carries the head of a lamb surrounded by a cruciform halo, or nimbus, and is terminated as a design by a scroll on which is written *Agnus Dei*, "the Lamb of God," to signify that Christ is the sacrificial lamb who took away the sins of the world.

33A. The next shield bears insignia that relate to the institution of the Holy Eucharist. The composition consists of three loaves of bread on a paten with grapes below it to symbolize the consecrated elements of the Last Supper.

32A. The top shield carries the chalice of the Last Supper in symbolic design. Holy Thursday is called the Birthday of the Chalice. On the partly exposed host at the top of the chalice are three Greek letters, *IHC,* which are the first three letters of the Greek word for Jesus.

31A. The uppermost shield at the right is reminiscent of the events of the Garden of Gethsemane, including Judas' betrayal and St. Peter's defense of Christ. The lantern on the shield is symbolic of the events of that night.

30A. The next shield is devoted to the episode in Pilate's court when Jesus was scourged and his kingship mocked. The shield displays a reed and two scourges.

29A. The last shield recalls the events of the outer court of Pilate where the cock crowed when St. Peter denied the Lord. The design in the shield is called the Petrine rooster and is symbolic of repentance and vigilance.

The next six shields of this third series are located directly over the altar and represent the crucifixion on Calvary and Christ's death, burial, and resurrection.

19A. The first shield carries the sacred nails, the hammer, and the pincers, such as were used when Christ was crucified. They are often called the *Arma Christi,* or the heraldic arms of Christ.

18A. On the next shield are other instruments used at the Crucifixion: the spear with which the centurion pierced Christ's side; the sponge on a reed offered to quench his thirst; and the inscription placed on the cross, here drawn as a scroll with the letters, *INRI* (originally written in Latin, Greek, and Hebrew), which stands for *Jesus Nazarenus, Rex Judaeorum,* "Jesus of Nazareth, King of the Jews."

17A. The design on the top shield at the left stands for the Crucifixion. A realistic crown of thorns encircles a Latin cross on which, in large Greek capital letters, are *CHI RHO SIGMA,* the first two and last letters of the Greek word *Christus* ("the Anointed One, the Messiah").

16A. On the uppermost shield at the right is a traditional symbol of Christ, the pelican. According to legend it feeds its young with its own blood and hence, with mystical significance, the pelican is an emblem of Jesus who shed his blood for mankind.

15A. The shield following is composed of two more instruments of the passion: the jar of ointment used in Jesus' burial and a linen cloth shaped in a formal design below the jar. This linen symbolizes the shroud in which Joseph of Arimathea wrapped the body of Jesus Christ as He was laid in the tomb.

14A. The last shield carries the banner, or oriflamme, of the Resurrection. On the top of the staff is a small cross enclosed in a circle; the narrow banner with a long cross unfurls itself around the standard.

The remaining colored shields are located on the Epistle, or south, and Gospel, or north, sides of the baldachin. Two smaller shields are held by the angels under each decorative terminal where the small double arches meet. These ten shields treat the four purposes, or effects, of the Catholic Mass.

35. On the south side from left to right, the first shield shows a design symbolizing the worship due to God. The gold crown with a cross and red

jewels acknowledges God's supreme perfection. The scepter and sword, each having silver, purple, and green colors, declare God's dominion over all, and the red flame beneath the design denotes man's absolute dependence on Him.

36. The second is devoted to the homage of praise and of thanksgiving due to God. This purpose of the Mass is symbolized by a musical instrument—the golden lyre on a green field has a red cross on its silverlined base and five strings of silver with red tops.

37. The third, a violet shield, expresses the expiatory purposes of the Mass. A red yoke with green cords and two silver scales is balanced on a gold cross enframed by a silver and red circle. The cross grows out of a green tree trunk with intertwining roots.

38. In the fourth shield the design stands for the Mass as a sacrifice of petition celebrated with the intention of promoting on earth the greater glory of God and obtaining assistance and every spiritual advantage of men. The design is a gold vase of fruit—three yellow pomegranates with green leaves, traditional symbols of prayer. The Greek letters *alpha* and *omega*, the beginning and the end, are on the vase itself. Two natural violets in balance are placed on each side of the vase to denote the virtue of humility.

On the Gospel (north) side of the baldachin are four more shields, identical both in location and in significance to the four just described. The designs of this second group, however, are different in their elements, taking their inspiration from world-famous objects of Celtic art, suggesting the position of St. Patrick as patron of the cathedral.

39. Reading from left to right, the first shield in white carries a huge gold chalice with green jewels which closely resembles the Irish chalice of Ardagh of seventh-century origin. A large silver host with the monogram of Christ in it and surrounded by a flowing red glorial arises from the chalice.

40. The design of the second shield in green denotes praise and thanksgiving. A harp fills the shield; its frame is silver with gold strings and red on the interlaces of its design. A single gold shamrock fills out a lower corner of the shield. The design of the harp draws its inspiration from that shown on the seal of the Dublin Museum.

41. The third shield is in violet. A gold cross of equal proportions fills the shield; its fourteen jewels are green. The design is based directly on that of the Cross of Cong (AD 1123). In back of the cross appears a crown of thorns, and at the center of the cross is a representation of a heart.

42. The fourth shield conveys a symbolical idea of petition. On a red field is an open book with a green and gold marker across its white pages; the clasps and book binding are in gold. Three silver arrows are seen behind the book. The book and arrows are symbols of prayer, and the choice of a book in this design was made with reference to the famous Celtic illuminated Gospel of St. Columbkille, called the Book of Kells, written in the seventh century.

43. On the Epistle side of the baldachin the angel holds a shield on which is a conventional design of the sun at dawn, a ring encircled with a spangled border. Above the sun are the Latin words, *Ab Ortu* ("from the rising...")

44. On the Gospel side the shield of another angel has on it a design of the setting sun—a raised ring with two circular depressions around it. Above this

design are the Latin words, *Ad Occasum* ("... to the going down [of the sun]").

The baldachin serves to focus the worshiper's attention on the high altar, the culminating point of the entire cathedral. Running around the four sides of the altar is a Latin inscription composed of quotations from St. John. It reads: "This is everlasting life, that they may know Thee the only true God and Him whom Thou hast sent, Jesus Christ. Take courage, I have overcome the world. Peace I leave with you, my peace I give to you: not as the world gives do I give to you. Abide in my love."

On the frontal at the center of the altar is a decorative motif, the bark of Peter, symbolic of the Church. Carved in low relief, the design depicts St. Peter seated at the stern of a small boat whose rudder he guides; in his right hand are the two keys of the apostolic primacy. On the sail of the ship is a chalice. The oriflamme flying from the mast is called the Resurrectional Banner, and the boat sails through conventional waves of the ocean in which small fishes are swimming.

Charles D. Maginnis, the architect and designer of the altar and baldachin, began studies of the project in 1930. Work was suspended during the depression years, and resumed in 1939. The entire project, from baldachin to details of the altar, was made possible by a contribution from a donor who has remained anonymous.

The Sanctuary

*W*ithin the sanctuary on the north side of the church, the marble statue of St. Patrick stands on a bracket of the nave pier. The saint is wearing a chasuble, chief vestment of the Mass, and an ancient miter. He holds a book of the Holy Gospel and a large shamrock sprig. Shamrock leaves also decorate the canopy of Gothic tracery above the figure. The piece was executed by John Angel, the sculptor who designed the statuettes of the baldachin, and the same anonymous donor presented this statue of its patron to the cathedral.

Two strikingly ornate carvings are focal points of the sanctuary amd integral parts of the highest religious ceremonies of the cathedral. The archbishop's throne, the chair the archbishop occupies during solemn functions within the church, is set in the north wall of the sanctuary screen, its pointed canopy, rich with bas relief figures of the Archangel Michael and others, rising thirty feet above the floor. The back of the chair itself includes statuettes of St. Peter and St. Paul, and the archbishop's heraldic insignia.

The pulpit is to the right of the communion rail, at the south corner of the sanctuary. It was designed by Renwick himself and made of Carrara marble taken from the quarry that supplied the columns of the Pantheon in Rome. Octagonally shaped, the pulpit has a base composed of eight columns of Siena marble. Five corners have canopied niches that hold figures of St. John, St. Peter, St. Patrick, St. Paul, and St. Andrew. The tester, or canopy, rises above the pulpit, decorated with pomegranates, grapes, lilies, oak leaves, and other designs of symbolic significance to the Church.

Running between the pulpit and the statue of St. Patrick, the marble communion rail encloses the sanctuary to a length of over fifty feet. Religious processions enter the sanctuary through a central bronze gate showing kneeling angels. The rail itself is designed with thirteen niches containing two-foot-high statuettes of saints of special significance to the sacrament of Communion.

The Crypt

The crypt lies beneath the high altar, reached by a marble stairway behind the altar and separated from the subfloor sacristy by a bronze door. The remains of Archbishop Hughes were transferred from the vault in old St. Patrick's Cathedral in 1883 to this most appropriate final resting place. In the crypt are also entombed John Cardinal McCloskey, Michael Augustine Corrigan, John Cardinal Farley, Patrick Cardinal Hayes, and Francis Cardinal Spellman, as well as two former rectors—Monsignor Michael J. Lavelle, the legendary priest who served the cathedral for fifty-two years, and Bishop Joseph E. Flannelly. The doors to the crypt are open for public viewing on select dates, such as All Souls' Day and certain anniversaries.

Way up in the distant recesses of the sanctuary ceiling, over one hundred feet from the floor, hang four flat-crowned, red ecclesiastical hats, called *galeros*, each having two sets of fifteen tassels that are each about five feet long. Part of the official cardinal's insignia dating from the mid-thirteenth century, the hat is conferred on appointment to the cardinalate and worn only at the College of Cardinals in Rome. On the death of a cardinal this insignia of his office is placed at the foot of the catafalque and afterwards suspended over his tomb.

The galeros of St. Patrick's include, closest to Fifth Avenue, the hat of the first American cardinal, John McCloskey. Next hangs Cardinal Farley's, then that of Cardinal Hayes—the beloved Cardinal of Charity—and last, Cardinal Spellman's, which will, incidentally, be the last galero to be hung in the cathedral. Among other ceremonial reforms undertaken by the Church in the late sixties, the tasseled cardinal's hat was eliminated and replaced by a smaller, more functional version. It was this hat that Cardinal Cooke received on his appointment in Rome.

Above the cardinals' hats at the topmost intersection of the ceiling moldings is a symbol of the Holy Spirit, a dove surrounded by sunrays, calla lilies, the rose, and palm leaves.

The Organ

Original plans for the cathedral called for two organs at either end of the church, which would collectively or separately serve the two choirs to be used. The grand, or gallery, organ is located in the first bay of the nave between the two towers, just below the rose window at the Fifth Avenue entrance. It is immense, which explains why the term *grand* is applied to it, and is set in a richly molded choir gallery crafted of ash. This gallery, which can hold up to 100 singers, rests on an iron beam capable of supporting 100 tons. The organ is forty-six feet long and twenty-eight feet high. The longest pipe is thirty-two feet and runs horizontally rather than vertically across the gallery; the smallest are about one-half inch.

The chancel organ is seen to the immediate left of the main altar, and was designed to accompany the chancel choir when the cathedral had two choirs. It was and is still used to play the verses of a hymn while the gallery organ plays improvisations between the verses. Approximately one-fourth the size of the gallery organ, the chancel organ proved too thin to support congregational singing if used by itself, and a third instrument — the echo, or antiphonal organ — was introduced to enhance the chancel organ. Placed in the south triforium, it sounds directly into the crossing, and it is this organ that is most clearly audible to the congregation in the nave.

The gallery organ is considered one of the finest such instruments in existence, and is used for frequent recitals of sacred music as well as to establish an ineffable mood of worship. Shortly after St. Patrick's opened, the builder of the organ, Mr. Jardine, gave a demonstration of its potential to a group of 500 ticket-holding guests. The audience marveled as he produced the sound of claps of thunder and the rolling away of the sound into the distance, the hissing sound of furious rain, and a musical roar so powerful that "if the listener will take his place at the other end of the church and hold a hat or cane lightly suspended in his hand, he will feel it vibrate in such a way as to produce the sensation of a mild electric shock."[1]

St. Patrick's continues to grow. For over a century the building has evolved and been improved. Wood gave way to marble and bronze, a flat wall was opened to the graceful sweep of the Lady chapel, the glorious stained glass and carvings piece by piece assumed their places and enhanced the whole. Successive archbishops have furthered its construction, improved its appearance, and left their special imprint. St. Patrick's today follows a more truly Gothic design than did the cathedral of 100 years ago and has come closer to an ideal plan.

Chapter 7:
The Twentieth Century

*T*en decades have worked extraordinary changes on St. Patrick's. Designed as a splendid tribute from man to God, the cathedral was to have been first and foremost a working church. It remains so, but is in addition a stellar tourist attraction as well as a symbol of permanence in a particularly dynamic setting.

The twentieth century St. Patrick's serves at least two congregations: the five priests assigned to the church say Mass, administer sacraments—from baptism of the newborn through extreme unction to the dying—and offer spiritual succor to those who consider the cathedral their parish church. Catholic residents of New York from Forty-fourth to Fifty-ninth streets between Third and Seventh avenues go to confession and "make visits" at the cathedral. If St. Patrick's ran bingo games (which it does not), locals would attend in much the same way that they attend any parish church.

But St. Patrick's neighborhood is no longer a residential district; a second, larger congregation exists in the horde of office workers who spend most of their workdays under the shadows of the spires of St. Patrick's. Noonday Mass, particularly on Catholic holy days, is filled with transients who will return home to Good Shepherd or Holy Name parish located somewhere in the city.

As a tourist attraction, St. Patrick's, although overshadowed by the towered complex across Fifth Avenue, is secured in the knowledge that, by city standards, Rockefeller Center is Nouveau York.

The size and grandeur of the working parish of St. Patrick's belie its church activities, which are essentially no different from those found in any Catholic church. There is a Senior Citizens Club, at which older parish members meet to play bridge, socialize, and work at crafts projects; an Al-Anon group for the family members of alcoholics meets regularly, as does a Debtors Anonymous club for any beset by gambling problems; and for those interested in finding out more about the Catholic religion, there are classes daily. An active and energetic volunteer group, made up largely of people who work in midtown New York, serves as the nucleus of parish workers. Obviously, most are Catholics, but the cathedral aura encourages nonsectarian participation as

Overleaf: Detail from window of the Lady chapel — Madonna and Child, designed by Paul Woodroffe after a window in the cathedral at Chartres. (Right) This nineteenth-century photograph shows the cathedral outlined in electric lights, compliments of the New York Edison Company as a promotion to sell the idea of electrification.

(Above) St. Patrick's Day mass, 1979. (Below) Cardinal Cooke leading the procession around the cathedral prior to celebrating the 100th Anniversary mass.

(Above) Cardinal Cooke greets well-wishers at the annual St. Patrick's Day parade. (Below) Marchers fill Fifth Avenue for the St. Patrick's Day parade.

The World's Largest Cathedrals

MAXIMUM CONGREGATION

St. Peter's, Rome	54,000
Milan Cathedral	37,000
St. Paul's, Rome	32,000
St. Paul's, London	25,600
St. Petronio, Bologna	24,400
Florence Cathedral	24,000
Cathedral of Notre Dame, Antwerp	24,000
St. Sophia, Constantinople	23,000
St. John Lateran, Rome	22,900
Notre Dame, Paris	21,000
St. Patrick's, New York	18,696
Pisa Cathedral	13,000
St. Stephen's, Verona	12,400
St. Dominus, Bologna	11,400
Cathedral Vienna	11,000
St. Mark's, Venice	7,000

well. One does not have to be Roman Catholic to learn. The common ground seems to be a fondness for St. Patrick's. A charismatic prayer group composed of individuals who choose to merge their individual feelings of devotion meets daily to offer prayers for communal intentions. Here again, a religious spirit rather than a single denomination is the bond between members of the group.

St. Patrick's is also an employer to more than thirty people. The custodians, ushers, musicians, electricians, and administrative office staff are not dissimilar from other corporate employees. Working conditions are undoubtedly more unusual than those at Metropolitan Life, but there is undoubtedly as much routine on either job.

A perfectly acceptable and traditional Christian practice was the rental of pews to the congregation. Agreeable all around, families were assured of "their" pews and the Church picked up some extra revenue. In the scrambling for completion, family pews at St. Patrick's were sold in perpetuity, with an annual rental fee required to keep the franchise in the family.

As times changed, the status of being a pew-holder dimmed and going to church became less a social function and more a religious one. New generations did not much care where they sat, and the time-honored custom of the family pew went the way of upstairs and downstairs maids.

Pew #11 is still held and the rental paid for yearly by the Butler family (among whose earlier members was the founder of Marymount College), the original holders of that pew.

Bennett Cerf, in his autobiography *At Random*, recalls the move into the Villard Houses behind St. Patrick's. The houses were a U-shaped complex of five separate dwellings built for the Villard family. The Villards lost their money and were forced to dispose of the handsome building. The five houses were sold individually, and in the early 1940s one was purchased by Joseph P. Kennedy, Sr.

According to Cerf—and it must be borne in mind that he was a gifted storyteller—a chance meeting with a monsignor assigned to the cathedral blossomed with such instant cordiality that on hearing of Random House's search for office space, the monsignor called Kennedy and directed him to sell the house to Bennett Cerf at no profit to himself, which he did.

A more believable version of the same story suggests that Kennedy agreed to sell at cost, but in fact doubled his money. The price of the property to Random House was $420,000 in 1946. When Random House resold the property in 1969, it received $2.5 million.

Two commercial enterprises have been largely—albeit indirectly—responsible for structural renovations to the cathedral. In 1947, Best & Co., an elegant department store, was being constructed across Fifty-first Street on Fifth Avenue. Blasting for the foundation caused a large block of stone to fall from the roof of the cathedral to the street below. No damage was done, but the accident alerted the church to the possibility of deterioration, and renovations were undertaken.

Best's was not to survive on the Avenue, and in the late 1960s, the property was sold to a consortium headed by Aristotle Onassis. The project this time was Olympic Towers, and again blasting was scheduled. Now the cathedral looked to its interior; there were deep lines across the roof—cracks? Scaffolding was built and a floor was constructed between ceiling and church below. The deep lines proved to be merely a century of dirt, which was sandblasted away.

In 1912, the newly consecrated Cardinal Farley returned to the cathedral from Rome and, in a city welcome that rivaled the demonstrations for Admiral Dewey and Theodore Roosevelt, hundreds of thousands of people celebrated his homecoming. In typical New York fashion, the welcome was spontaneous and grew as the cardinal proceeded to the cathedral from downtown. No ceremony had been planned, but his arrival coincided with the first electric illumination of the cathedral's exterior. A heavy hailstorm, also unplanned, caused more confusion and crowding at the jammed cathedral. Cardinal Farley had come home.

The first time the doors of St. Patrick's were left open all night was for the coronation of Pope Pius XII on 12 March 1939. A radio broadcast beginning at midnight was carried by the four major networks and was heard at St. Patrick's. Bishop Fulton J. Sheen delivered the commemorative sermon.

During World War II, standees were not allowed at St. Patrick's, although in previous years overflow crowds at Sunday services filled the aisles. As a precaution against possible air raids, however, the aisles were cleared to prevent any congestion in case a hasty exit was necessary.

More than 50,000 people attended eleven masses and three benedictions celebrating the end of World War II.

Winston Churchill, on the last day of a two-month vacation in this country in 1946, startled noonday visitors at St. Patrick's when he and Cardinal Spellman emerged from the door connecting the cathedral with the cardinal's residence. Churchill strode up one side of the cathedral and back down the other, prayed for a few minutes at one of the side altars, then left as abruptly as he had arrived.

Midnight Mass at St. Patrick's was televised for the first time on Christmas Eve 1948. All three networks — NBC, CBS, and ABC — carried the live broadcast.

St. Patrick's was the first American church to be inscribed by name on the floor of St. Peter's Basilica in Rome. The Vatican ordered the inscription to coincide with the beginning of the 1950 Holy Year and the visit of Cardinal Spellman, who was reportedly unhappily surprised at how far away the inscription was from the papal throne. All inscriptions are placed according to church size, and St. Patrick's ranks twelfth in the world.

St. Patrick's has appeared in many New York films, but it served as stage for only one, a 1955 Warner Brothers epic entitled *Miracle in the Rain*, which starred Van Johnson and Jane Wyman. The movie, a bittersweet tale of doomed wartime romance, is remembered by the staff of St. Patrick's more for its weather effects than for its plot. The movie lovers met at St. Patrick's and

Lighting

A battery of eighty switches controlled the illumination of St. Patrick's. Soft, low-wattage bulbs were used to send a diffused light throughout the massive interior; the intent was a suggestion of inner light, as though the altar or crucifix or statue actually glowed light. Sanctuary illumination had to be designed to provide ample light for reading liturgical passages without casting shadows distracting to the congregation and to the officiating priest.

The lighting panel was modernized in mid-fifties and ten silent buttons now regulate interior and exterior lighting as well as signal lights coordinating the choirs as to the correct time to respond.

The lighting system in the cathedral is used approximately sixteen hours a day and is inspected daily by teams who replace, repair, and maintain the lights.

sidewalk hydrants were tapped to provide atmospheric rain on cue. Thousands of gallons of water were sprayed against the great doors of the cathedral, and all shooting was done from ten at night to dawn.

An irate father tried to delay his daughter's wedding in St. Patrick's by throwing four stones at the cathedral windows in 1957. No damage was done to the windows or to the ceremony, which had taken place two hours before, but the father of the bride was arrested for disorderly conduct.

Leopold Stokowski conducted the Metropolitan Opera orchestra in another cathedral first, an orchestral concert with a three-dollar price tag. All receipts went to a program for retarded children originally started by Cardinal Spellman. The concert, held in 1965, continued the ecumenical movement started by Pope John XXIII. Worshipers unaware of or uninterested in the concert came and went amid the ovation and two encores accorded the eighty-eight-year-old Stokowski.

Twelve nuns lay down in the aisles of St. Patrick's during the morning Mass services to protest against the escalating war in Vietnam. Seven of the nuns were arrested, although no charges were filed. The prostration was intended as a symbol of Vietnam war dead, and the demonstration a request for Cardinal Cooke to withdraw as military vicar of the United States Army.

(Above) Pope Paul VI, with Frances Cardinal Spellman, outside St. Patrick's during the pontiff's 1965 visit to New York.

In 1971, an African folk mass was sung in the cathedral to benefit an impoverished diocese located in the West African country of Upper Volta. The mass was offered to the lone beat of four African drummers who accompanied the words of the traditional Latin service.

Dimensions of the Cathedral

THE INTERIOR

306 ft.	Length
124 ft.	Total width
96 ft.	Breadth at the nave and sanctuary (exclusive of the chapels)
48 ft.	Nave: width of nave from pier to pier
108 ft.	height of nave transept and sanctuary vault
24 ft.	Aisle: width between nave piers and side chapel walls
54 ft.	Height of side aisle
144 ft.	Transept: length
96 ft.	width
108 ft.	height
95 ft.	Sanctuary: length at level of the clergy choir
107 ft.	from communion rail to center of apse pier
48 ft.	width
14½ x 26 ft.	Windows: typical clerestory
28 x 58 ft.	transept clerestory
13½ x 27 ft.	aisle windows (above chapels)
26 ft.	rose window (diameter)
290 sq. yds.	Lady chapel: area
56½ ft.	length
28 ft.	width
56 ft.	height
21 ft.	The flanking chapels, semioctagonal (diameter)
64 ft.	Ambulatory: length
15 ft.	width
48 ft.	height
12 ft.	High altar: length
4 ft.	width
17 ft. 8 in.	Baldachin: (between the four piers)
12 ft. 6 in.	maximum width (front and rear) maximum depth
38 ft.	pier openings from sanctuary pavement to top of the arches (front and rear elevations)
57 ft.	height (from the sanctuary pavement to base of the statue of St. Michael)
32 ft. 6 in.	to top of roof

THE EXTERIOR

332 ft.	Exterior length
174 ft.	Exterior breadth
132 ft.	General breadth
32 sq. ft.	The towers at base
136 ft.	Height of the square towers
54 ft.	Height of octagonal lantern
140 ft.	Height of spire
330 ft.	Total height from street to top of spire
156 ft.	Central gable, Fifth Avenue
23 ft.	Width of typical bay
104 ft.	Height from ground line to eaves (50th-51st streets)
138 ft.	To top of grand pinnacles of buttresses, side elevations
12½ ft.	Depth of wall at central portal
30 ft. wide 30 ft. high	Central portal
48 ft. wide	The transepts (above 50th Street and 51st Street entrances)
170 ft. high	(to top of crosses)

Chronology

1810: Census shows population of the United States to be 7,239,000, including 60,000 immigrants and 1,200 slaves.

Purchase of the site of the cathedral, March of that year.

1812: June, Congress declares war on England over Canadian territories.

1820: US population of 9,638,000, including 98,000 immigrants. New York has 124,000 people.

1830: US population of 12,866,000, including 150,000 immigrants.

1840: US population of 17,069,000, including 600,000 immigrants.

1841: The first screw-propeller ship, *Princeton*, was built. There were forty-seven public schools in New York City.

1850: US population of 23,191,000, including 3,200 slaves and 1,700 immigrants.

A new cathedral is proposed by Archbishop Hughes.

1852: *Uncle Tom's Cabin*, by Harriet Beecher Stowe, is published; in a little over a year, 1 million copies are sold.

1853:

Plans for the cathedral begun by James Renwick.

1858: Construction of Central Park is underway. The committee of the National Association of Baseball Players invites the New York Board of Aldermen to witness a match between the Brooklyn and New York players at the Fashion Race Course near Flushing. Macy's Department Store opens. Oil is discovered in Titusville, Pennsylvania.

Laying of the cornerstone by Archbishop Hughes.

1861: Confederates fire on Fort Sumter.

1863: The New York *Daily News* loses postal privileges and is suspended from publication for eighteen months because of its violent antiwar policy.

1865: President Lincoln is assassinated. Mark Twain's *Celebrated Jumping Frog of Calaveras County* becomes an immediate favorite.

1867: Alaska is purchased.

1868: In one of the earliest attempts at a New York municipality, a city commissioner complained of the growing suburbs, saying, "More than one and one half million people are comprehended within the area of this city and its immediate neighborhood, all drawing sustenance from the commerce of New York, and many of them contributing but little toward the support of its government.... the difficult question of taxation of non-residents... now exists." The first modern apartment house in New York is built at Eighteenth Street and Third Avenue.

1872: James Abbott McNeill Whistler exhibits his *Arrangement in Black and White No. 1, My Mother*. Immigration this year is almost 500,000, chiefly from Germany, England, and Ireland.

1874: First electric streetcar in New York City.

1875: Churchill Downs is founded at Louisville, Kentucky.

John McCloskey becomes first American cardinal.

1876: Alexander Graham Bell demonstrates his telephone. The National League is founded; teams represent Boston, Chicago, Cincinnati, Louisville, St. Louis, Philadelphia, and New York.

1877:

The cathedral is open to visitors, although not yet in use.

1878: The State legislature passes a law to create a pension fund for disabled and retired policemen in the City of New York. The Third Avenue Elevated opens from South Ferry to Forty-second Street. The first NYC telephone directory is issued—there are no numbers; all calls are made by name. The Metropolitan Stock Exchange is organized by "those interested in stock speculation in a small way."

Fair held in St. Patrick's, which is complete except for the spires.

1879: Thomas Edison demonstrates his incandescent lamp. Frank W. Woolworth opens up a 5¢ store in Utica; it fails but a second enterprise, a 5 & 10¢ store with a wider variety of merchandise, becomes a success.

Cathedral is officially opened by John Cardinal McCloskey.

1880: US population is 50,156,000, including 2,812,000 immigrants.

1881: The US Supreme Court holds that income tax levied during the Civil War is constitutional.

1884: The Washington Monument is completed.

1888:

Spires of cathedral finished.

1890: New York Gov. Theodore Roosevelt calls Tolstoy "a sexual and moral pervert" and the US Postal Service prohibits mailing of his *Kreutzer Sonata*. The Plaza Hotel opens.

1890: US population is 62,948,000, including 5,247,000 immigrants.

1891: James A Naismith invents basketball. New York's Mayor Grant tells the city that "the problem of rapid transit is no closer to solution than it was two years ago . . . the proper cleaning of streets is also a subject of great importance with which little progress has been made." New York has more asphalt than London or Paris.

1898: Spanish-American War is declared.

1900: Orville and Wilbur Wright fly at Kitty Hawk, North Carolina. King C. Gillette begins to manufacture disposable razor blades.

1900:	US population is 75,995,000, with 3,688,000 immigrants. New York population: 3,437,000.	
1906:		First mass celebrated in the Lady chapel.
1908:	The Model-T Ford is put on sale at $850.	
1910:	US population is 91,972,000, with 8,795,000 immigrants.	St. Patrick's is dedicated by Archbishop Farley.
1912:	*Titanic* sinks.	
1914:	Panama Canal is officially opened to traffic.	
1915:	Taxi industry begins in New York City; fare is 5¢.	
1917:	Russian Revolution overthrows Czar Nicholas and Communism is established. US enters war against Germany.	
1918:	Daylight Savings Time begins. Armistice is signed.	
1919:	Eighteenth Amendment (Prohibition) is ratified into law.	
1920:	US population is 105,711,000, with 5,736 immigrants.	
1930:	US population is 122,775,000, with 4,017,000 immigrants. 1,300 banks close. Sinclair Lewis is awarded the Nobel Prize for Literature. The Empire State Building, then the tallest building in the world, is dedicated and opened.	New organ dedicated.
1936:	King Edward VIII abdicates his throne for "the woman I love." Franklin Roosevelt's election victory over Alf Landon is the most decisive in American history.	Eugenio Cardinal Pacelli, soon to be Pope Pius XII, presides at the twenty-sixth anniversary of the consecration of the cathedral.
1939:	Albert Einstein advises Roosevelt that nuclear fission is possible, and that two German physicists have already achieved it. Roosevelt declares the US neutral in European war.	Francis Cardinal Spellman installed as archbishop of New York.
1940:	US population is 131,669,000, with 528,000 immigrants.	
1942:	United Nations is formed. Rent control is established in war industry areas. 110,000 Japanese, including 75,000 American-born, are interned as security risks. First jet plane is flown.	Consecration of the new high altar. New windows installed in the apse.
1945:		Exterior renovation precipitated by excavation for Best & Co., the department store.
1949:	NATO is formed. US troops are withdrawn from Korea. Eleven Communists are fined and imprisoned for conspiracy to overthrow the American government.	New bronze doors are blessed.

1950: US population is 150,697,000, with 1,035,000 immigrants.	
1956: Desegregation begins in the US. Interstate Highway System is voted.	New windows installed in the clerestory.
1960: US population is 179,325,000, with 2,515,000 immigrants.	
1965: Pres. Lyndon Johnson escalates Vietnamese War. Electricity fails in the Northeast. Soviet astronaut makes first space walk.	The first papal visit to the United States; Pope Paul VI celebrates Mass at St. Patrick's.
1968: President Johnson announces that he will not seek reelection. Martin Luther King is shot in Memphis; Robert F. Kennedy is shot in Los Angeles. Three US astronauts achieve lunar orbit.	Installation of Archbishop Cooke.
1969: American combat toll in Vietnam now higher than in Korean conflict, with 40,000 dead. Woodstock festival establishes solidarity of American young. Man walks on the moon.	Terence Cardinal Cooke welcomed upon returning from Consistory.
1970: U.S. troops enter Cambodia.	Restoration of main altar, baldachin, and altar in Lady chapel; cathedral is air conditioned.
1971: Twenty-sixth Amendment gives eighteen-year-olds the right to vote.	Exterior lighting of steeples and facades is installed.
1973: Skylab is launched into orbit.	Complete restoration of cathedral; Blessed Sacrament chapel is renovated, prompted in part by excavation for Olympic Towers and fear of falling debris caused by blasting.
1974: Watergate scandal forces resignation of President Richard Nixon.	Opening of parish house and new meeting rooms.
1975: War in Vietnam ends.	New shrine of St. Elizabeth Ann Seton.
1977: Panama Canal treaty is signed.	New shrine of St. John Neumann.
1979: Resumption of diplomatic relations with mainland China.	Cathedral celebrates centennial year.

Footnotes

Chapter 1
1. Moses King, *King's Handbook of New York City 1893*, p. 383
2. *Ibid.*, p. 33

Chapter 2
1. Brawn, Henry, *The Most Reverend John Hughes*, p. 192

Chapter 3
1. *The New York Times*, Oct. 2, 1910, p. 2
2. John M. Farley, *History of St. Patrick's Cathedral*, p. ii
3. *Ibid.*, p. iii
4. *Ibid.*, p. vi
5. *Ibid.*, p. vii
6. *Ibid.*, p. x-xii
7. *Ibid.*, p. xii
8. *Ibid.*, p. xiv
9. *Ibid.*
10. *Ibid.*, p. xv
11. From "The Diary of a Little Girl in Old New York," as quoted in *New York: Sunshine and Shadows* by Roger Whitehouse, p. 205
12. John A. Kouwenhoven, *The Columbia Historical Portrait of New York*, p. 295
13. As quoted in *Manhattan Moves Uptown*, Charles Lockwood, p. 236
14. *The New York Times*, July 26, 1858, as quoted in *The Iconography of Manhattan Island*, W. Phelps Stokes, p. 1877
15. As quoted in *Rockefeller Center: Architecture as Theater*, p. 7
16. John M. Farley, *History of St. Patrick's Cathedral*, p. 69
17. James D. McCabe, Jr., *Lights and Shadows of New York Life, Or, Sights and Sensations of the Great City*, p. 445-446
18. *Ibid.*, p. 497
19. *Ibid.*, p. 447
20. *Appleton's New York Illustrated*, 1869, as quoted in *The Iconography of Manhattan Island*, W. Phelps Stokes, p. 1933
21. James D. McCabe, Jr., *Lights and Shadows of New York Life, Or, Sights and Sensations of the Great City*, p. 444
22. As quoted in *The Upper Crust*, Allen Churchill, p. 146
23. As quoted in *Manhattan Moves Uptown*, Charles Lockwood, p. 207
24. James D. McCabe, Jr., *Lights and Shadows of New York Life, Or, Sights and Sensations of the Great City*, p. 208

Chapter 4
1. *The New York Times*, June 25, 1895, p. 9
2. Henry Cleveland, "North American Review," as quoted in *Bricks and Brownstone*, Charles Lockwood, p. 103
3. Arthur Gilman, "North American Review," as quoted in *Bricks and Brownstone*, Charles Lockwood, p. 103
4. *The New York Times*, July 12, 1858, p. 8
5. *The New York Times*, August 16, 1858
6. *The New York Times*, August 16, 1858
7. John M. Farley, *History of St. Patrick's Cathedral*, p. 116
8. Charles Lockwood, *Bricks and Brownstone*, p. 105
9. John M. Farley, *History of St. Patrick's Cathedral*, p. 118
10. *Ibid.*
11. *Ibid.*, p. 119
12. *Ibid.*, p. 122
13. *The New York Times*, August 16, 1858
14. John M. Farley, *History of St. Patrick's Cathedral*, p. 123
15. *The New York Times*, August 16, 1858
16. John M. Farley, *History of St. Patrick's Cathedral*, p. 122

17. *Ibid.*, p. 122
18. *Ibid.*, p. 123
19. John M. Farley, *History of St. Patrick's Cathedral*, pp. 125-126
20. *The New York Times*, August 9, 1860, p. 8
21. *The New York Times*, May 7, 1875, p. 8
22. *The New York Times*, October 23, 1878
23. *The New York Daily Tribune*, November 2, 1878, p. 8
24. *The New York Times*, October 23, 1878
25. *Journal of the Fair for the New St. Patrick's Cathedral*, October 23, 1878
26. *The New York Times*, May 18, 1879, p. 10
27. *The New York Times*, October 2, 1910, p. 8
28. *Ibid.*
29. As quoted in *Alive and Well in New York City: St. Patrick's Cathedral*, May 1978, p. 11
30. *The New York Daily Tribune*, September 25, 1885, p. 8
31. *The New York Daily Tribune*, May 26, 1879, p. 1
32. *The New York Times*, May 18, 1879, p. 10
33. *The New York Times*, May 2, 1879, p. 5
34. *Ibid.*

Chapter 5
1. *The New York Daily Tribune*, October 23, 1878, p. 5
2. *The New York Times*, August 24, 1875, p. 2
3. Old Testament, Genesis: 14, v. 18
4. *The New York Times*, April 19, 1903, p. 33
5. *Architectural Record*, Volume 21, June 1907, p. 428

Chapter 7
1. *The New York Times*, May 23, 1879, p. 5

Bibliography

Andrews, Wayne. *Architecture, Ambition, and Americans.* New York: Free Press, 1947.

Archbishopric of New York. *St. Patrick's Cathedral.* New York: 1942.

Balfour, Alan. *Rockefeller Center: Architecture as Theater.* New York: McGraw-Hill, 1978.

Birmingham, Stephen. *Real Lace: America's Irish Rich.* New York: Harper & Row, 1973.

Black, Mary. *Old New York in Early Photographs.* New York: Dover, 1973.

Brann, Henry. *The Most Reverend John Hughes.* New York: Dodd, Mead, 1892.

Burnham, Alan. *New York Landmarks.* Middletown, CT: Wesleyan University Press, 1963.

Cerf, Bennett. *At Random.* New York: Random House, 1978.

Churchill, Allen. *The Upper Crust.* Englewood Cliffs: Prentice-Hall, 1970.

Collins, J.F.L. *Collins' Both Sides of Fifth Avenue.* 1910.

Farley, Most Rev. John M. *History of St. Patrick's Cathedral.* New York: Society for the Propagation of the Faith, 1908.

Grafton, John. *New York in the Nineteenth Century.* New York: Dover, 1977.

Gumaer, A.H. "The New Lady Chapel at St. Patrick's Cathedral, New York," *Architectural Record* 21 (June 1907).

Hassard, John. *Letters of John Hughes.* New York: D. Appleton, 1866.

Humphrey, Effingham P. "The Churches of James Renwick, Jr." Master's thesis, New York University, 1942.

Moses King, ed. *King's Handbook of New York City 1893* vol. 1, 2d ed. Reprint. New York: Benjamin Blom, 1972.

Kouwenhoven, John A. *The Columbia Historical Portrait of New York.* New York: Harper & Row, 1972.

Lockwood, Charles. *Bricks and Brownstone: The New York Row House, 1783-1929.* New York: McGraw-Hill, 1972.

————*Manhattan Moves Uptown.* Boston: Houghton Mifflin, 1976.

Lyman, Susan. *The Story of New York.* New York: Crown, 1975.

McCabe, James D., Jr. *Lights and Shadows of New York Life, Or, Sights and Sensations of the Great City.* New York: 1872.

New York Historical Society. *New York: Then and Now.* New York: Dover, 1976.

Reed, Henry Hope. "Catholic Church Architecture in America." *Thought* 31 (Autumn 1956).

Richmond, Rev. J.F. *New York and Its Institutions, 1609-1872.* New York: E.B. Treat, 1872.

Simon, Kate. *Fifth Avenue: A Very Social History.* New York: Harcourt Brace Jovanovich, 1978.

Shaw, Richard. *Dagger John.* New York: Paulist Press, 1977.

Stokes, W. Phelps. *The Iconography of Manhattan Island.* New York: Robert H. Dodd, 1926.

Webster's Guide to American History. Springfield, Massachusetts: G. & C. Merriam, 1971.

Whitehouse, Roger. *New York: Sunshine and Shadows.* New York: Harper & Row, 1974.

Withey, Henry and Elsie. *Biographical Dictionary of American Architects (Deceased).* Los Angeles: New Age Press, 1956.

Illustration Credits

Photographs are by Leland A. Cook, Herbert Wise and David Frazier unless otherwise indicated.

Chapter 1
page 20 Courtesy of The New-York Historical Society; page 23 The Museum of the City of New York

Chapter 2
page 27 The Museum of the City of New York; page 28 (both photos) Culver Pictures

Chapter 3
page 31 The Museum of the City of New York; page 33 Culver Pictures; pages 36-37, 40-41, 42 Courtesy of The New-York Historical Society; pages 43, 44, 45 (both photos) Culver Pictures; pages 46-47 Courtesy of The New-York Historical Society

Chapter 4
page 51 The Renwick Collection of Columbia University; page 53 Culver Pictures; page 54 The Museum of the City of New York; page 56 Courtesy of The New-York Historical Society; page 60 The Museum of the City of New York; page 61 (all photos) Archives of St. Patrick's Cathedral; pages 62, 63 The Museum of the City of New York; page 64 The Renwick Collection of Columbia University; page 69 The Museum of the City of New York; page 70 (left) Culver Pictures, (top) The Museum of the City of New York

Chapter 7
page 143 The Museum of the City of New York; page 150 Francis Miller, Life Magazine © 1965 Time Inc.

Index